JUNG
and the
QUAKER WAY

Jack H. Wallis

QUAKER HOME SERVICE
LONDON

First published May 1988
Reprinted January 1992
This edition February 1999
by Quaker Home Service
Friends House, Euston Road, London NW1 2BJ

The cover illustration shows the rose window in the
cathedral at Orvieto. It is taken from the book *Rose
Windows* published by Thames & Hudson and is
reproduced with the permission of the publisher and the
photographer Painton Cowen. The line drawings on the
title page of each section are by Clifford Creative Design

CONTENTS

Introduction to the Second Edition

Ten years have passed since the original publication of Jack Wallis's influential work, *Jung and the Quaker Way*. The long standing popularity of the book has assured its republication in this, its third edition. It is now published as a Quaker Classic, a label which recognises both the timelessness and the time-bound qualities of this probing and pragmatic text.

In 1994 Britain Yearly Meeting agreed its revised version of *Christian Faith and Practice*, its Book of Discipline and the principle book of the Religious Society of Friends in Britain. Now renamed *Quaker faith and practice*, the latest edition kept many of the well-loved and well-used quotations, but also added new contributions.

Advices and Queries, the essence of *Quaker faith and practice* were also reworded. New emphases are evident in *Quaker faith and practice*, most clearly in sections on sexuality, parenthood, bereavement and divorce.

Jack Wallis's analysis of Quakerism needs to be read with an understanding that it reflects British Quakerism of the mid 1980s. As an example, when considering Quakers' orientation away from evil and towards good, he counts the indexed references to darkness and to light in *Christian Faith and Practice*. In *Quaker faith and practice*, the ratio of these numbers is inverted. The threads of Jack Wallis's comparison rely absolutely on such an analysis, and so a mere replacement of references to *Christian Faith and Practice* with those in *Quaker faith and practice* would not be faithful to the author's ideas and understanding.

Jung and the Quaker Way is nevertheless a tool for Quakers today. Wallis's central thesis, that Jungian psychology and Quakerism have commonalities which are mutually informing, remains relevant. Jung's writings can potentially enlighten Quakers' experience of spirituality, enhancing the sacramental nature of their daily lives. Furthermore, the last section of the book, 'Response', has some unusually practical suggestions to make about such approaches, and usefully interprets the experience of meeting for worship.

Jack Wallis died in 1998, in the process of preparing *Jung and the Quaker Way* for this new edition. He was a much loved member of Winchester Meeting who wrote extensively, particularly on counselling and social welfare, drawing from his work with the Marriage Guidance Council and the National Association of Citizens' Advice Bureaux. He also wrote *Findings, an enquiry into Quaker Religious Experience* which was published by Quaker Home Service in 1993.

Emily Miles

Editor's note: Rather than amend the original text with fresh references you will find editorial revisions at the back of the book.

ACKNOWLEDGEMENTS

This publication has two aims. The first is to consider the relevance for Quakers of what Jung had to say about the religious attitude to life. The second aim is to consider the relevance of Quaker faith and practice for those who are interested in depth psychology. The book is written in the conviction that these two areas of concern can illuminate and enrich each other both by their similarities and their differences.

Jung died in 1961, aged 85. His Complete Works have been published in English for the Bollingen Foundation by Pantheon Books in New York and by Routledge and Kegan Paul in London. They amount to 18 volumes of material written mainly between 1910 and 1946. Two years after Jung's death, Collins and Routledge published his autobiographical *Memories, Dreams and Reflections*. Many of Jung's interviews with journalists have been issued in *Jung Speaking* (Thames and Hudson, 1978) in which he comments informally on questions of popular interest and concern. There are also volumes of his correspondence now in print.

All this presents a formidable amount of material to work from or to refer to. The task has been greatly simplified by two substantial anthologies of extracts from his Collected Works. The present author gratefully acknowledges the permission of the editors and publishers for the use of these two principal sources of brief quotation from the Complete Works for a critical assessment of Jung's views on religion, expressed in his own words. The two anthologies are:

Psychological Reflections: an anthology of the writings of C. G. Jung, selected and edited by Jolande Jacobi. New York: Pantheon Books, vol. 13 in the Bollingen Series, and London: Routledge & Kegan Paul in Ark Paperbacks. *Jung: selected writings*, selected and introduced by

Anthony Storr. London: Collins (Fontana) and Princeton, N.J., USA: Princeton University Press.

Detailed references to Jung's text in the Complete Works are given by both editors of these anthologies and are therefore not repeated here. There is a large literature on many aspects of Jung's work by his associates, students and followers published in America and some in Britain. Some of these are included in the Bibliography.

The author also acknowledges his indebtedness to authors and publishers of books listed in the Bibliography which, over the years, have contributed indirectly but substantially to the general frame of reference for the present critical assessment and summary.

Personal thanks are also due to those psychologists, psychiatrists, psychotherapists, social workers, counsellors and clergy with whom I have worked as a counsellor and particularly in the selection and training of Marriage Guidance counsellors and tutors. Their expertise, experience and differing views were as stimulating as they were helpful and constructive.

Finally, thanks are due to individual members of the Religious Society of Friends (Quakers) both locally and at Friends House in London for their encouragement and direct help, in particular to Dr W. H. Allchin, Clifford Barnard, Jo Farrow and John Withrington. They are not, of course, responsible for the book's deficiencies or the author's opinions.

JACK H. WALLIS

PART ONE

The Context

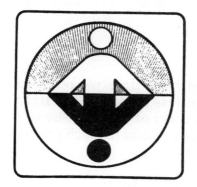

'Be ready at all times to receive fresh light from whatever quarter it may come; approach new theories with discernment. Remember our testimony that Christianity is not a notion but a way.'

from 'Advices' (1964)
    Church Government §702, III

'It is high time we realized that it is pointless to praise the light and preach it if nobody can see it. It is much more needful to teach people the art of seeing.'

    C. G, Jung
from *Psychology and Alchemy*, para 14

1 Organized Religion and the Living Spirit

What has Jung to say to Quakers?

Throughout his long life, Carl Gustav Jung was committed to the task of healing. That is to say, his work was directed towards health in its proper sense of wholeness, a harmony and integration of the inner and outer aspects of life and an active and developing unity of body, mind and spirit. He was the son of a Swiss pastor (specializing in oriental languages) and was trained in medicine. He saw personal wholeness as the true goal of human growth, in contrast to a one-sided over-emphasis on the physical, the intellectual or the spiritual.

As is well-known, Jung parted company with Freud mainly because of Freud's insistence on the supremacy of sexuality and his denigration of the part played by the spiritual side of life.

In this book we are concerned with those aspects of Jung's work and teaching that are most relevant to Quaker faith and practice. He maintained that no human being can stand a life without meaning and he considered neurosis to be the pain of those who have not yet succeeded in finding the true meaning of their life. It was in this sense that he said that religions are (or should be) therapeutic. Not sanctity or righteousness but health, or wholeness, is our proper goal. This seemed to him as self-evident as that an acorn should become an oak or a kitten a cat. He asserted that any true religion should be founded on experience, not on dogma, doctrine or a dutiful faith. For him, as for Quakers, both faith and practice are based on experience and arise from it. He believed that religions are an essential part of an individual's striving towards wholeness (especially those he called the greatest religions of mankind, Buddhism and Christianity).

Jung was not a religious writer in the conventional sense

but a wise, original and intuitive observer of inner human experience and interpreter of its meaning. He was not interested in theological debate or intellectual theorising whether religious, philosophical or occult. Indeed, he regarded theories as a cloak for ignorance so far as human nature is concerned (reminding one of the Buddha's dismissal of theoretical speculation as not tending towards enlightenment). He called the soul (psyche or spirit) 'the eye destined to behold the light'.[1] He means 'destined' in the sense that the nose is destined for smelling, the ear for hearing. That is what they are for.

Spiritual reality is apprehended through the soul of the individual, not through the mind or intellect. As we shall see shortly, he believed that in the West our capacity for spiritual understanding has dangerously declined. He has much to say on how and why this blindness has afflicted us and, in this same sense, he and his followers are uniquely qualified to 'teach people the art of seeing'.[2]

It is worth pausing here briefly to consider the everyday, figurative use of words connected with light and seeing. We use *see* to mean know or comprehend, *looks as if* means gives a wrong impression. To *throw light* on something is to explain it, to make it intelligible. To *look at* means to consider. To *make him see* is to persuade him to accept an idea or a *view*. We call a person of intelligent intuition a person of *vision*. But a *visionary* is someone who is unrealistic, airy-fairy. *Look,* we say when we mean listen. *Don't you see?* we exclaim when we mean Can't you understand?

Jesus called his disciples 'the light of the world'.[3] Five hundred years earlier, the Buddha called true spiritual understanding by a term that is always translated *enlightenment.* St John asserted that 'God is *light*'[4] and St Paul explained that now we 'see through a glass darkly'.[5] This symbolic use of *light* occurs many times in both Old and New Testaments, as reference to any comprehensive concordance will show. Do you, we ask, *see* the point?

Still using this same symbolism, we have to bear in mind that light throws a shadow. Indeed, light has no meaning without darkness, or good without evil. 'The world is not a

4

garden of God the Father; it is also a place of horror,'[6] wrote Jung, a view not often expressed, perhaps, in a Quaker context. The Buddha placed the irrefutable fact of suffering first of the Noble Truths, and as the foundation of the other three. Moreover, the brighter the light the darker the shadow and the more we shall behold. To change the metaphor, if we eat of the tree of understanding we cannot expect to remain in a Paradise of blissful ignorance.

A last point about light: the light we seek in a spiritual sense may be either a destination (like the light at the end of a tunnel) or on the contrary a lamp-post that lights the way, enabling us to see our path more clearly and avoid pitfalls. For the Buddha, enlightenment was the supreme goal. For Quakers, the Inner Light shows us the way.

There are (among Quakers as elsewhere) those who are by nature faithful followers rather than seekers or explorers or inquirers. As Jung pointed out, where no one asks, nobody need answer. For them, it is enough to follow loyally the trodden way, the accepted path. But for most of us that is scarcely possible today. We cannot shut our eyes to all doubt and unbelief or believe the unbelievable or achieve faith as an act of will or on authority.

Jung's contribution to religious, psychological and spiritual understanding becomes increasingly relevant in the chaotic confusion and unrest of present-day life in the West. This hardly needs elaboration as it is all too obvious. We have only to read or hear or watch the latest news of what has happened, is happening, is likely to happen or might happen or could happen. The problems that disturb us seem so intractable, as we pin our hopes on political or social solutions or cling desperately to outmoded beliefs. Jung did not offer any final solution but showed the way by which problems might be approached. 'We moderns (he wrote) are faced with the necessity of rediscovering the life of the spirit; we must experience it anew for ourselves.'[7] He wrote those words more than fifty years ago. What has since happened around us and is happening now gives them an even greater urgency, as is the case with almost all he wrote on the topic we are considering.

In spite of all the evils that surround us, as a relentless

and inescapable shadow of all the good, Jung maintained that humanity has not grown wickeder but has far greater means of expressing the propensity for evil. Our spectacular advances in technology, in instant communication, in the menace of war and civil unrest, in nuclear destruction—all these, not always evil in themselves, have hugely increased the scope for evil among us. Christian civilization, in Jung's view, has been unable to keep pace and has 'proved hollow to a terrifying degree: it is all veneer, but the inner man has remained untouched and therefore unchanged.'[8] Attempts to deal with such momentous problems by social, scientific or political means have been largely ineffective because they overlook the fact that life with a meaning can be lived only by individuals, not by the State or the Party or any other collective. Our social goals, Jung believed, promote only collective and individual illusions, without ministering to the needs of the individual. Better conditions do not make us better people, only more comfortable. This over-emphasis on externals and neglect of the inner needs of the individual make progress largely hollow. 'Is modern man (asked Jung) in danger of 'losing the life-preserving myth of the inner man which Christianity has treasured up for him?'[9] and he asked whether we realize what the consequences would be.

We rely on political solutions to our problems but progress is frustrated by the adversarial polarity of party politics by which all evil is seen to reside in the other party, all good in one's own. From this follows the relentless drive for power (that is, for election) by all possible means in a rivalry in which the objective even of external social improvement is replaced by the necessity of winning votes. 'The goal and meaning of individual life (which is the only real life) no longer lies in individual development but in the policy of the state'.[10]

Any effective collective solution to social problems, in Jung's view, can arise only from a change in individuals, never from legislation, or propaganda, mass meetings or violence. But the individual is increasingly ignored and his and her inner needs neglected, leaving them suffocated and deprived of responsibility, suggestible in the mass but personally reduced to a non-entity. Jung stressed the danger in these developments. 'Great conglomerations of people are always the breeding ground of psychic epidemics'.[11] 'All human control comes to an end (he wrote) when the individual is caught in a mass movement',[12] and individuals are then all too easily, he said, reduced to the level of the beast or demon that lurks within.

And yet, says Jung, the individual is 'the only direct and concrete carrier of life'.[13] He explained: 'A million zeros joined together do not, unfortunately, add up to one. Ultimately everything depends on the quality of the individual',[14] yet we moderns tend to think always in collective terms.

How far are these developments and the resulting suffocation of the individual personality by collectives reflected in the Quaker way? Before we consider this, we should hear what Jung has to say about the part played by the Churches (that is to say, religious organizations) in the changing relative importance of State and individual. He maintained that religion is of unique importance in its traditional function of safeguarding the integrity of the individual. But on the other hand, in the West the Churches have largely failed in this health-giving function through concerning themselves with externals and leaving the individual without support. 'The worldly-minded mass man looks for the numinous experience in the mass meeting', he wrote, and added 'Even Church Christians share this pernicious delusion'.[15]

He criticised the Churches' reliance on unreflecting belief in tradition and collective conventions, reinforced (one must surely add) by all the techniques of suggestion, repetition, suitable music, ritual, ceremonial, vestments, obsolete and much-loved language. The effect of suggestion (whether in religion or secular advertising) is to by-pass the critical judgment and induce acceptance, a psychological process akin to hypnosis or 'brain-washing' and widely used in politics, advertising and propaganda to induce credulity, especially at election times.

The Churches, said Jung, 'do not appear to have heard of the elementary axiom of mass psychology that the individual becomes morally and spiritually inferior in the mass'.[16] Elsewhere he asked 'Did the feeding of the five thousand bring him any followers who did not afterwards cry with the rest "Crucify him"?'.[17]

Jung believed that religion should provide the most effective and perhaps the only counter-balance to the fatal tendency to mass-mindedness which he saw as the greatest menace of our time. Events since his death have surely endorsed his warning.

Unfortunately, the Protestant Churches (in his opinion) have failed in two other ways. One of these is their rigid paternalism which has always undervalued the feminine; the other is a dependence on external features of collective worship and intellectual hair-splitting at the expense of an intuitive understanding of human nature put at the service of individual Church members. A further point, implied rather than clearly expressed in Jung's work, is a reluctance to accept the reality of evil and to over-emphasize the image of the loving Father and creator of 'all things bright and beautiful'.[18] Jung claimed that God also has a dark side. In Anthony Storr's helpful introduction to his book of selections from Jung, he suggests 'The decline in conventional Christian belief . . . is related to the fact that the Christ-image . . . excludes both evil and the feminine',[19] and cannot therefore any longer symbolize wholeness.

The question of evil concerned Jung in several contexts, as we shall come across in later chapters. For the present, it will serve to introduce the relevance for Quakers of what we have been discussing and to ask ourselves how far Jung's views on the part played by the Churches applies to our own Church. We see ourselves as one of the Churches: the second part of the Book of Discipline is called *Church Government*.

In the first volume entitled *Christian Faith and Practice in the Experience of the Society of Friends*[20] there is (as Friends well know) an excellent comprehensive index to the 677 quotations. Under the index heading 'Light, Inner' there are 29 references. Under 'Darkness and Dryness' there are

7. Under 'Evil' there is not one. Clearly one must not make too much of this, especially as there is no entry under 'Good' either. But does it, perhaps, give a hint about the general orientation away from evil and towards the good?[21] To put it bluntly, do we Quakers, in our loyalty to the personality of Jesus 'exclude evil' (as Anthony Storr wrote) from our consideration? No one, of course, denies the existence of evil. But how far do we see it as the inevitable counterpart to good, as dark is necessary to light and as a coin cannot have a head without a tail? We acknowledge 'that of God' in everyone. Is there 'that of evil' too? Can we speak of wholeness and yet exclude the ugly, the cruel, the evil propensities in all human nature?

William James[22] coined a vivid term for certain kinds of religion that do indeed eliminate evil from their purview. He called them Healthy Minded. Perhaps the best known of these is Christian Science. Others are more like a pseudo-science than a religious body, such as for instance, the Science of Thought, optimistic, positive, operating by suggestion, constructive, beneficient in intent of an occult or spiritualistic nature. The Buchmanite Oxford Group was of a similar character, more definitely moralistic than scientific and thoroughly Healthy Minded. Such movements seem to be more popular in America than in Europe and some of them there have a huge following.

Systems that depend mainly on suggestion are, in the long-run, precarious aids to the conduct of life or spiritual development, though attractive to those who want quick results. They 'work' for a while by a species of magic in the way that placebos work in medicine even though they are based on deception. Magic is effective till we know how it is done. People who embrace Healthy Minded systems of whatever kind are usually euphoric, uncritical, zealous, optimistic, enthusiastic and not susceptible to discussion, much less open to doubt. To deny the existence of evil or failure gives one a heady feeling. But such systems and their effects seldom last.

Is there perhaps an element of Healthy Mindedness among Quakers? Do we tend sometimes to deny the same status to evil as to good? Can we accept both Inner Light and Inner Dark? We speak sometimes of the Inner Voice and indeed experience it as a reality, as the prompting of God within our heart. Can we accept the possible reality of a second Inner Voice also? Or do we shut our ears like those monkeys that 'Hear no Evil' and 'See no Evil'? We shall return to these questions later, not with answers, but to see them from other angles.

How true is it to suggest (as Anthony Storr has done) that the Churches exclude the feminine? Quakers have a good record in this respect, though today we have our feminists and their critics. Are we, perhaps in subtle ways, a paternalistic Church as, according to Jung, many Christian Churches are?

It has long been customary, from ancient Jewish times, to posit God as universal Father, not Mother. Not until 1950 was the bodily assumption of Mary into Heaven proclaimed as a dogma by Pope Pius XII, an event regarded by Jung as 'the most important religious event since the Reformation'.[23] Perhaps on the whole we Quakers are today less concerned than most other Christians and Jews with the first person of the Trinity. Our image of Jesus (who proclaimed 'I and the Father are one'[24]) is inevitably masculine. But the Holy Spirit is free from gender. Is it possible that we are slowly and painfully shifting the focus of our commitment from the second to the third person of the Trinity, from the Redeemer Son to the Holy Spirit? If that should be so, we are likely to move into closer association with the inner spiritual aspect of other religions of our complex society, receiving and giving fresh light as we approach each other, not rejoicing in their differences and strangeness but widening and deepening our religious understanding, with discernment and with humility.

How far is it true of Quakers as of other Protestant Churches (according to Jung) that we over-rate and over-emphasize externals (our practical, social, organizational concerns) to the disadvantage and detriment of our inner, spiritual needs? Jung felt it was significant that the Protestant authorities changed 'the Kingdom of God is within you' to 'among you',[25] as though to keep clear of anything within and keep to externals. How far do Quakers tend to see evil as always something outside, never inside? Traditionally we have a good record of identifying practical, material and social injustices that need our active concern. Can this tendency be overdone so that it limits a sensitivity to inner needs of others and of ourselves also? Quakers pioneered many good works that are now undertaken by other voluntary or by statutory organizations. On the whole, do we become alert to inner religious and spiritual needs that are neglected, or do we look ever farther afield over the world for unmet external needs?

These various questions arise directly from Jung's observations. Our response remains our own responsibility. There is, however, no mistaking what he felt to be the primary function of a religion, namely to minister to the inner needs of the individual.

2 Psychology, Worship and the Shadow

'Healing may be called a religious problem'[1] wrote Jung. How can psychology help us with it?

Jung believed psychology has a particular responsibility for guiding us back to our inner nature, now that religion is so much concerned with externals. Indeed, he wrote 'All that is left today is the psychological approach.'[2] He saw psychology and religion as complementary and the task as urgent. It cannot be achieved through ever-increasing factual or theoretical knowledge but through intuitive understanding and experience. To understand a person one should 'lay aside all scientific knowledge of the average man and discard all theories . . . The positive advantage of *knowledge* works specifically to the disadvantage of *understanding*.'[3] Healing and self-knowing come through experience, not through the intellect. There is a difference between knowing a person and knowing about a person. We may know a lot about individuals and then, when we meet them and get to know them, we find they are very different from what we expect. We begin to know people only when we experience them. Then we affect each other. Our subjective opinions and feelings are enlivened and the individual becomes real to us. In connection with religion, also, Jung maintained 'We cannot understand a thing until we have experienced it inwardly'.[4] Only then do we really know it.

This distinction between knowing and knowing-about marks an important division between two categories of psychology. We can roughly separate them as being scientific and objective or therapeutic and subjective—looking outward or looking inward, impersonal or personal.

Scientific psychology has greatly expanded our knowledge of human nature. It is the approach used, for example, in aptitude and intelligence testing, laboratory research and experiment, diagnosis of mental illness, assessment of mental handicap, in vocational guidance and sales techniques, in clinical uses of aversion therapy and operant conditioning, in selection and assessment procedures, in management, advertising and propaganda. In all these, objective facts are obtained about people, from as large a sample as is practicable, or some technique is applied to people as though they are objects. The procedures are objective and exact. The personal likes and dislikes of the operator are irrelevant, as are value-judgments. As for the recipient, he or she need only co-operate and follow instructions. In some instances (propaganda and sales techniques) even this may not be necessary; people are acted upon for a purpose without their being aware of it. This sounds rather unethical, but it may be to their advantage and the effect may be one they ardently want, as when we go to the dentist.

Formal religious services and social ceremony and pageantry are external in this same sense. To some extent they are also scientific and objective and collective. All this rests on what is well-defined, organized, classified and (usually) involves counting and measurement and timing. Subjective judgment and emotional responses interfere with such procedures and distort results. When people's feelings and their value judgments are treated as objects to be used for a purpose (as in advertising and political broadcasts) they are not in any way helped towards personal wholeness or psychological well-being.

In the early part of Jung's professional life (mostly before 1914) he was engaged in original scientific work, in experiments, in investigating misreading, assessing mood disorder and (later) in psychological typology. But his main interest and most original work was not in this category but in the other, healing.

It was, of course, the towering genius of Freud that pioneered the most thorough, painstaking and original enquiry into the workings of the inner life of individuals and led him to formulate the theory and establish the practice of psychoanalysis, which he believed would be best remembered as the science of the unconscious. Jung (as mentioned in the first chapter) turned his attention increasingly to an area of observation and enquiry that Freud regarded as of secondary importance and little interest. This is the part of human concern that is expressed through imagination, phantasy, ideals, meanings and values and in religion. This shadowy region of activity is creative and original and individual and does not lend itself to scientific appraisal, to measurement or even to any precise classification. In psychoanalysis, dreams (which Freud called the royal road to the unconscious) tend to be interpreted in terms of wish-fulfilment or compensation. For Jung, dreams represent imaginative constructions, a kind of internal drama free from the restrictions and conventions of waking life, autonomous creations (somehow creating themselves). Sometimes they occur in the context of the dreamer's experience and unsolved problems, sometimes they represent the expression of neglected sides of the personality, sometimes they emerge, like fairy tales or myths from our collective, unconscious inheritance.

To any busy, practical, active person, living mainly in 'the real world' of news and shopping and money and sport and sex and entertainment, trying to find work and somewhere to live and eat and sleep—to all this side of us, the inner area of Jung's chief interest may seem unreal, up in the clouds and irrelevant. That is just why it concerned him, because it is so much neglected. How we love to be busy (most of us) and are shame-faced at being idle. Is not the conventional reply to a query about retirement, 'Oh, I'm busier than ever'? Who says 'Now there is time to think, to listen, to look, to absorb, to idle or meditate'?

'From the standpoint of intellect (wrote Jung) everything else is nothing but phantasy. But what great thing ever came into existence that was not at first phantasy?'[5] Jung warned all who would listen of the danger of over-emphasis on externals and neglect of the inner life that is so characteristic of our age of triumphant technology and aggressive commercialism. The danger is immense. It is the psyche of man, he pointed out, that makes wars. They are not natural disasters. 'Complete absorption in the external world becomes an incurable affliction (he wrote) because no one can understand how one can possibly suffer from oneself'.[6] The penalty we have to pay for this unbalance is that the neglected, shadowy inner world is, as it were, dammed-up and may explode at any time in neurotic illness or collective epidemics of fanaticism, destructiveness, violence, revolution or war. For the inner life is potentially our greatest help or greatest danger. Individually, according to Jung, the unconscious part of our own personality may be our best friend or greatest enemy. We shall see presently something of the bearing this has on the Quaker way of living and of worship. But first we should consider the second category of psychology, that which is concerned with healing, wholeness and the subjective, inner life of individuals.

Like the first category, this is also expressed in different ways. The most skilled and intensive are Freudian psychoanalysis and Jungian analytical psychology. Other forms of psychotherapy are less rigidly separated into 'schools' of method and less rigorously focused onto the unconscious parts of the personality than in a formal analysis. The insight and the practice of the psychotherapist have influenced social workers of all varieties and also the many voluntary workers in organizations that seek to help individuals with their personal problems and difficulties. Many years ago the Methodist minister Leslie Wetherhead pioneered the introduction of psychology into pastoral work, though this was originally based more on the so-called classical psychology than on analytical therapy. Today there is a flourishing movement of Pastoral Psychology and within the Church of England a formal system of Clinical Theology. The Marriage Guidance organization was founded by a small professional group, most of whom were Quakers. It gradually developed an increasing concern with emotional and psychological aspects of the relationship (not without some disquiet among those mainly concerned with morality) as did many other voluntary and professional social work organizations. At the Tavistock Institute a small group of social caseworkers worked under the supervision of analysts and developed a high degree of therapeutic competence. By now the concept of counselling has been widely developed in a great variety of contexts, some medical, some social work and some in education and training and in management. The word has as yet no generally accepted definition and therefore no uniform approach to the selection, assessment, training and supervision of counsellors. But in any form, it is directed towards *individuals* and what their problems and difficulties mean to them emotionally and is based therefore primarily on a non-directive and tolerant listening and on the intuitive skill of the counsellor.

In the United States the psychotherapist Carl Rogers and his school of Non-Directive Counselling changed the focus of interest away from the external problem facing people in trouble to the impact that the situation was making on the individual. Carl Rogers showed how uniquely individual are the meanings that personal difficulties have. What is a trivial concern to one person may be shattering to another. People often cope courageously and effectively with troubles that seem overwhelming to anyone else, and yet are defeated by what to another seems just ordinary. Our most intractable problems and difficulties have some subjective significance for us, usually unconscious.

It seldom occurs to us that the problem resides in our own personality as well as coming upon us from outside. The external aspect is obvious, in the full light of day. Our inner reaction to it lies hidden in the shadow. And it is this inner aspect that determines whether or not we can cope with it. This is why it so often happens that good advice is no help. The difficulty generally lies not in knowing the solution but being able to apply it. When one is dealing with emotional difficulties like keeping one's temper or feeling defeated, anxious or jealous, there is always a pitfall facing an untrained counsellor. This is to discover what the individual is unable to do and then to advise him or her to do it.

All this affects a moral approach to behaviour. What an individual ought to do may not be possible until its inner significance has come into the light. Until it has, it is (properly speaking) not a problem of morals but of psychology. This is clearly of crucial significance in pastoral work.

Whoever tries to help people with their personal problems, whether in psychology, religion, education, morals, social work or ordinary life, may all too easily assume that other people can alter their feelings and their emotional attitudes if only they would. A further error arises from what may be called pop-psychology. This is the widespread belief that if you can offer someone a plausible explanation of why they feel the way they do, they will then feel differently. We are so used to thinking in straightforward terms of cause and effect that we assume our minds work along the same predictable lines. This disregards the subjective part of the situation.

Especially when we are concerned with some emotional difficulty or some problem of relationship, we need to bear in mind an individual's unique inwardness, the irrational aspect that neither of us understands and which therefore cannot be changed to order. Jung neatly summed up the only way of helping. Because each individual is unique, 'no counsellor, however wise, could prescribe the way that is uniquely right for them. Therefore we have to teach them to listen to their own natures'.[7] In this way they may grasp what is occurring in their lives.

We now turn to the bearing of these issues on the Quaker way—a relevance that is not, I fear, immediately obvious. By 'the Quaker way' I include our way of worship, of conducting business meetings, our administrative structure, our religious orientation and corporate attitude and our general moral and ethical consensus. In this task I am relying to some extent on my own experience of a small number of different Meetings but chiefly on George Gorman's splendid summary, based on his long, perceptive and extensive experience of Quaker Meetings in Britain and abroad. This was published in 1973 with the title *The Amazing Fact of Quaker Worship*.

How far do Quakers recognize the fundamental distinction between those things that are objective, external and practical and, on the opposite hand, the subjective, personal and spiritual? Meeting for Worship is the heart of the Quaker way and is I believe unique among the Christian Churches. The absence of formality, of a priesthood, of special furnishing, music and vestments is uniquely helpful in fos´•ring the inner, spiritual and individual yet corporate basis of the gathering. An essential freedom arises from silence, stillness and simplicity, a freedom for the inner spirit of each member to express itself inwardly, with little interruption. A gathered meeting attains a spiritual corporateness that, if all goes well, leads to what George Gorman called a 'lending of our minds to one another'.[8] This simple phrase captures the combination and harmony of both the individual and the corporate quality of verbal ministry, words that come from the heart as well as from the head, the soul as well as from the mind. Indeed, that is one feature that distinguishes Quaker ministry from a thoughtful contribution to a discussion. It is a short soliloquy in which the speaker somehow speaks on behalf of the others as well as to them and does so from an inner urge to say something that has arisen out of the silence and furthers what was said before.

There are, of course, occasions that fall short of this, as George Gorman describes. There is the mini sermon, the healthy-minded reassurance that all is well, the anecdote that is perhaps of private interest but not connected with the meeting and out of context. Considering that a Quaker meeting provides a captive audience, that it is open to anyone to attend and that silence is a powerful temptation to the talkative, it is remarkable how seldom such difficulties occur. When they do, it will, I believe, be always found that the speaker is oriented outwards instead of inwards.

Underlying a gathered meeting there is, it seems to me, a corporate concentration on what Quakers call 'those things that are eternal' (namely spiritual truths and values) and an urge to reach a deeper and wider understanding of them. This is a healing experience in a special sense and gives to a 'good meeting' its very special character for those present who are spiritually in tune with it. Jung wrote of the moral effort of a surrender to some supreme value (Quakers would perhaps call it listening to the inner voice or being sensitive to the leading of the Spirit or of God). In this way 'a man may even catch a fleeting glimpse of his wholeness, accompanied by the feeling of grace that always character-izes this experience.'[9] (In today's idiom he would of course have written 'person', not 'man'). It may at first seem strange that he speaks of surrender and moral effort, for it is easy to think that silence is purely passive. But we have to make the effort to reach a gathered state, we may have to look hard to discern the light or listen attentively for the inner voice. What Jung can do for us is to help us see it clearly and more often. As Anthony Storr put it: 'Jung rediscovered God as a guiding principle of unity within the depths of the individual psyche'.[10]

At its best, a Quaker meeting makes the same discovery through an admitted and shared determination to help one another towards it. Jung recognized the importance of this moral effort and what can happen if it is lacking, even in a religious context. 'The more unconscious the religious problem of the future remains, the greater is the danger that man will misuse the divine spark within him for a ridiculous or demoniacal self-glorification'.[11] This is what may happen when religion is externalized in highly emo-tional collective gatherings.

Before we pass on to consider what Jung termed the 'shadow', we should briefly notice the distinction between an expertly managed therapeutic group (led by an analyst or psychotherapist trained in group work) and a Quaker meeting for worship. There are some similarities in the set-up of the two, though Quaker meetings are usually much larger. But the aim is not quite the same. The critical difference is the Quaker corporate religious surrender to a transcendent entity and a supreme value, however it is named. This is usually not an agreed part of the orientation of a therapeutic group, indeed it hardly could be if it were a psychoanalytic group. Moreover, the analyst conducting the group plays a vital, skilled and sensitive part in inter-preting the unconscious emotional interchange within the group. Nevertheless the direction towards wholeness (which Jung regarded as religious in character) is more clearly relevant in the therapeutic group than in the Quaker meeting where, of course, no one takes the part of the analyst.

From a psychological point of view this agreed orientation is a potent safeguard against unconscious rivalry within the meeting which, in the absence of a therapist, could be unhelpful or even destructive. The fact that the same orientation is carried into Quaker business meetings is valuable in just the same way and gives them, under the guidance of the clerk of the meeting, their special character. The ending of a Quaker Meeting for Worship with the announcements by the clerk is also psychologically sound, for while the purpose of the meeting is spiritual, wholeness requires a reminder that externals are real also and have to be dealt with openly. We cannot live permanently in the gathered state so appropriate and valuable for a spiritual purpose.

A brief warning is appropriate here on this question of groups with a religious and spiritual orientation. It is possible for enthusiasts to mistake the distinction mentioned earlier between external and internal aspects of the personality. We considered the errors that can arise from counsellors who muddle the two and try to treat internal, emotional issues by means appropriate to external problems, by advice or a technique or some form of manipulation. The same can happen with groups and can, with good intentions, produce havoc. The management of a group that aims to be concerned with the inner side of the personality requires skill, training, sensitivity and insight because the therapist will be facing a complex interchange among the participants of emotions that are not fully conscious. Unhappily, one does sometimes come across groups that meet for only a short period and are led by someone who thinks that success means stirring everyone up and then has not the ability to deal constructively with the resulting turmoil. This is a risky undertaking and sometimes a psychotherapist has to clear up the effect on some unfortunate participant. Meeting for Worship is a far better way to avoid such accidents and has effective built-in safeguards.

Jung's concept of the Shadow underlies these issues and the relation between psychology and religion. The popular idea of the unconscious is of a sort of emotional sink-basket where all kinds of disreputable urges are discarded. Another popular view is that the unconscious contains memories that cannot be recalled deliberately because they would be far too painful. For Jung, the shadow is 'the "negative" side of the personality, the sum of all those unpleasant qualities we like to hide'.[12] 'Negative' here does not mean only those qualities that are unconstructive. It means also something like a photographic negative which corresponds to a print exactly but is reversed, black being white, brightness being shadowy. This is a useful idea because it brings to our attention the important and little-understood fact that the qualities we show most clearly have their opposites in the unconscious. Qualities—not sins or traumatic experiences. Jung wrote that the shadow contains 'childish or primitive qualities which would in a way vitalize and embellish human existence, but convention forbids'.[13] It is thus not wholly bad. It is composed of primitive qualities considered undesirable by those around us and which were unacceptable to our parents and others in our most formative years.

Such qualities are sometimes valuable, constructive, even creative but had to be disowned because they were totally unacceptable in childhood. Many people get a second chance as they enter middle-age after the busiest years with work and family. And, either with the help of a therapist or through their own courage, allow their potential to develop and flower. They seem, as their friends say of them, to become a different person. For the shadow is not idle but sometimes thrusts itself upon our conscious attention. If its pressure is great and yet we cannot acknowledge the qualities it is trying to thrust upon us we are apt to get irritable and ill at ease.

This discomfort leads us to blame others for the very qualities we cannot accept in ourselves, (known in psychology as projection). Those qualities that make us hottest under the collar give us a hint that here is something in ourselves that we are unable to acknowledge. 'Everyone carries a shadow',[14] said Jung. Everyone? Everyone! Of course, this is a pill that is hard to swallow. It means accepting the unacceptable side of oneself. No wonder we look for scapegoats to blame.

Jung maintained that the personal shadow can be assimilated: that we can learn to recognize it when it thrusts itself upon us and not disown it. This is the path to wholeness, a religious as well as a psychological task. Indeed, it is an indispensable task. 'How can anyone (asks Jung) see straight when he does not even see himself and the darkness he unconsciously carries with him?'.[15] What he advocates is that we learn to accept ourselves and not deny or fight against those qualities that emerge from time to time within us and which we have learnt to disclaim. This is the way he put it: 'Christ espoused the sinner and did not condemn him . . . Love makes a man better, hate makes him worse—even when that man is oneself'.[16]

In psychotherapy a most important task is to enable a sufferer to accept himself (or herself), shadow and all. This is a difficult and often a lengthy process. Needless to say it will not be achieved if the therapist in the deepest part of him cannot accept his own personality. To the extent that he can, he will be able to accept his client—not necessarily what that client does but what he is, a fellow being with 'that of God'[17] within him and also with his personal shadow, which some Christians are apt to regard as being of the Devil. This, incidentally, is why to be effective any psychotherapist must have been through a training that brings him face to face with his own shadow, so as to acknowledge at least some of his own imperfection. (Needless to say 'he' once again means 'she' as well. There are probably more women than men psychotherapists and counsellors).

What has this to do with the Quaker way? Does our Meeting for Worship help us individually towards wholeness? Does it enable us to face some aspect of the personal shadow within, that part we are normally reluctant to face?

Can we accept our own dark side as well as our bright side? Or do we tend to back up one another in the belief that, because we are Quakers, we are exempt from having a shadow? Can we accept the idea that as Jesus accepted those who sinned, so should we learn to accept those who sin, including our own self? Can we accept the idea that to recognize our own shadow does not mean we condone our own frailty but that we can accept the sinner while acknowledging the sin?

Only through learning to accept their inner nature can men and women 'also learn to understand and to love their fellow men better'.[18] If that should sound like heresy to conventional Christian morality, one may hear what else he said on the same issue: 'I cannot love anyone if I hate myself.'[19]

Those who have difficulty in accepting the idea of a personal shadow as far as they themselves are concerned, whose knowledge of human nature is two-dimensional (that is, without depth), all too easily think that morality attaches to feelings, that hateful, hostile, cruel or greedy feelings are immoral. They do not, perhaps, realize that the feelings that arise in us are neither moral nor immoral, but neutral. The supreme importance of morality is the way we choose to act on our feelings. And we shall not be free to choose if we do not know what they are. 'There is no morality without freedom'[20] said Jung and, elsewhere, 'Freedom stretches only as far as the limits of our consciousness'.[21] In this psychological sense it can truly be said that love (that is acceptance) gives freedom, and freedom gives responsibility.

3 Feelings, Relationships, Values

Near the end of his life Jung wrote 'I have been compelled to say what no one wants to hear,'[1] so difficult is it for us to accept the unconscious counterpart to the world of consciousness. Has it become any easier for us now? In some ways it has. Everyone has heard of the unconscious (which Freud at first called the subconscious). We recognize those embarrassing 'Freudian slips' where someone says something different from what they intended and people laugh, knowing that they, too, can get caught out in the same way. We are familiar also with slips of memory that unhappily give an impression that we forgot something on purpose. Which of us has never felt the shame of forgetting a date, a promise, a gift, an anniversary, an appointment, a name? Then there is the unintended innuendo or the quip that misfires and gives offence and we hasten to explain 'Of course, I was only joking'. Some of these slips are trivial, some are hurtful and humiliating. 'It must be my unconscious' we say and laugh it off.

To most normal, sensible people there is something far-fetched in the thought that there really is a counterweight to the conscious world. Perhaps we can accept it as some kind of new mythology of mystery and magic, or some psychic Science Fiction or maybe just a phantasy of those 'trick-cyclists'. But the unconscious becomes a very different matter when Jung and others reveal the collective unconscious as the source of wars and revolutions, fanaticism and violent demonstrations and protests, or psychic epidemics of mass hysteria. Even the personal unconscious (the shadow) is not readily acceptable to most of us and feels somehow a rather degrading idea. It is a bit spooky to think we may have our own private dark corners, hidden even from ourselves.

Curiously enough, however, many everyday phrases suggest that we do have a suspicion that there is indeed another Me around, that we are not total masters in our own house, that there is both an I and a Me (or Myself). 'I was not myself that day—I was beside myself—I took a grip on myself—I lost control of myself—I pulled myself together just in time—I was lost in myself—I didn't trust myself'. All these simple expressions suggest that Myself and I can pull in different directions. We feel that I ought to be able to control Myself but sometimes cannot. When I is in control (excuse the grammar) we feel confident and we do not relish having a backseat driver. Sometimes we are conscious of two inner voices. One comes up with a good, kind or original idea or prompting, and the other finds excuses.

The unconscious, however, does not only make itself heard. It makes itself felt in unruly ways. We have to admit that emotion can, and often does, distort reason, and feeling can interfere with thinking. For instance, the letter we just cannot wait to write is probably ill-judged. Sometimes anger or jealousy or suspicion suddenly arise and we assume they are fully justified. 'Emotion (wrote Jung) . . . is not an activity of the individual but something that may happen to him'.[2]

The unconscious can be the source of inspiration and joy as well as of feelings that make difficulties for us. It may be a spring of love and beauty, of ecstasy even. Sometimes it presents us with our 'brain-waves', flashes of insight or understanding, brilliant ideas, answers to some problem that make us cry out suddenly 'I've got it!' and laugh. These surprises usually arise when we are not puzzling our heads or worrying but are thinking of something else or of nothing. The familiar advice to 'sleep on it' often gives the unconscious a chance to get to work. It does not always oblige, but sometimes it does, in its own time and its own masterly way. Then we can only say, 'How did I think of that? I've no idea. It just came to me'.

Our feelings (conscious and unconscious) are a prime source of energy, far more potent than our conscious will, which sometimes has some reluctance attached to it. Our feelings can supply drive, zest, inspiration, sometimes enabling us to endure difficulties, discomforts, dangers and fatigue. How else do mothers manage to carry the burden of a very sick and distressed child, day after day, night after night? There are latent resources of emotional strength and endurance within us that devotion can excite, enabling us to excel ourselves.

Feelings play so significant a part in our lives that the Freudian phrase 'pleasure principle' seems inadequate to explain the phenomenon. Such energizing may be pleasant or unpleasant, directed at the past (as with guilt or satisfaction) or the future (anxiety, ambition) or the present (joy, grief, anger, fear). Emotions may seem to be normal or abnormal (to oneself or to others), good or bad, praiseworthy or shameful, reasonable or unreasonable. They may arise in association with an event, with a person or an object. They may puzzle us by their intensity or inappropriateness so that we say 'I can't think why it upset me so much'.

In the form of a mood, some unconscious emotion may interfere with us and colour whatever we are doing, until it passes as mysteriously as it arose. This is so baffling that we search for a cause, the weather or news or something we have eaten or some incipient illness or we may attribute it to the stars or some psychological theory that we think accounts for it. It is disconcerting when a mood seems to make no sense. It makes us feel we are no longer in charge. Our thinking mind assumes it is always rational and is outraged or confused when irrational emotion muddies the water. In an age addicted to science and technology and the intellect it is hard to believe that emotions can happen to us without our knowing how or why.

The American neo-Freudian, Karen Horney, wrote of 'the queer fellow who lives your life'.[3] Perhaps this is going a bit too far and suggests he is always in charge. Jung expressed the same idea more gently: 'I happen to myself'.[4] Even that is hard to believe when, for instance, we fall in love. Suddenly life is transformed for us by the living embodiment of our inner ideal. We feel fated, spellbound, in ecstasy. Others may call us infatuated but to ourself it is heaven, magical, life-enhancing. Something of the same kind can happen to us from an idea (as it does to a poet) or a work of art or even from a building, a place, a view though these are usually transitory. Alas, though, we can fall in love disastrously with someone who has a fatal attraction for us and whom we dislike or fear, like the Belle Dame Sans Merci of Keats or the Dark Lady of Shakespeare's sonnets.

When considering Jung's ideas and discoveries in today's context, it is necessary to keep in mind that most of his work was written a generation or more ago. We should ask therefore how far the general public attitude to human personality has changed. Is the general 'climate of opinion' on the relative importance of inner and outer factors (and inner and outer experience) different from what it was when he was writing? Is the context the same now?

The most obvious and spectacular changes have undoubtedly been in science and technology rather than religion and the arts. In the former there have been breathtaking achievements but what can we say about any general interest in spiritual concerns? Today everyone hears about progress in computer science and its applications, space travel, genetic engineering, body scanning and a host of new electronic devices for entertainment and leisure, convenience and fun and communication. What is there in the way of progress towards wholeness of personality, psychic health or spiritual understanding? Can it be seriously doubted that the imbalance between inner and outer that Jung noted has greatly increased? Can there be such gains in the one scale without corresponding loss in the other?

Freud's ideas and discoveries aroused great interest in professional circles and the widest publicity was secured by their controversial nature, particularly around the subject of sex. Here at last there seemed promise of a science of human nature with ramifications into all the human sciences and professions.

What chiefly concern us here are the assumptions that we take for granted. For instance, we now realize (at least in theory), that unconscious feelings and attitudes may influence relationships and affect our strongest views. We

accept that many of our strongest convictions and prejudices stem from early childhood, from the attitude of our
parents, what they approved and disapproved of, and
what they did not even recognize in us.

Some psychological terms have now become part of our
daily vocabulary, such as subconscious, mother (or father)
fixation, Oedipus complex, ego, libido, repression, projection—from Freudians; inferiority complex, masculine protest, compensation, sibling rivalry, social interest—from
Adlerians; introvert and extravert, archetype, collective
unconscious, animus and anima—from Jungians.

Various psychological ideas and assumptions (mainly
from Freudians) became part of the social climate. Perhaps
the most notable was the sudden appearance (not without
scandalized opposition) of Sex as a topic and Sex Instruction as a scholastic subject. Matters that had hitherto been
kept strictly taboo came into the open—homosexuality, the
sexuality of women, sexual deviation, toilet training,
infantile sexuality, the meaning of dreams and phobias.
There has been an increasing understanding of the psychological importance of the relation of parents to their
children from infancy onwards and also between siblings.
The child has become an object and focus of interest. The
first five years of life are generally accepted as crucial for
the formation of lifelong attitudes. Child development has
become a specific branch of psychology. Rebellion against
parents and parent-figures is now popularly accepted as a
normal phase of development, as is hostility to authority of
any kind, to coercion or discipline.

Jung's influence in all this was not great. He did not
accept the Freudian scheme of development—the oral,
anal, genital and Oedipal phases. He was convinced that
the psychological disturbances of children arise in most
cases from unconscious problems of their parents. He
therefore directed treatment to them rather than to the
children. He took little part in the elaboration of theories of
child development.

Stemming initially from the work of Freud (not Jung)
most psychological interest has been focused on childhood

as the stage when the foundations of personality are formed. Today it is taken for granted that the psychological disturbances of adults are to be understood by reference to what went wrong early in life. In this sense it may be plausibly suggested that for Freudians the vital focus of interest lies in the past (in infancy and early childhood) whereas for Adlerians it lies in the future (our goal-directed purposes) and for Jung the focus lies mainly on the present situation. This is an over-simplification but it illustrates important differences of outlook. As far as Jung's views are concerned, one may be reminded of an observation by the Danish theologian Kierkegaard[5] to the effect that we understand life backwards but live it forwards. Yes indeed, but we should not neglect the present, where past and future meet.

Jung was scornful of ambitious and optimistic plans for developing the personality of children. 'The achievement of personality (he wrote) means nothing less than the optimum development of the whole human being'.[6] In other words it is our life task. He thought attention should be focused less on the child and more on the adults who were bringing him up because, as he pointed out, 'no one can train the personality unless he has it himself'[7] and 'We cannot correct in a child a fault that we ourselves still commit'.[8] I think he must have felt a little exasperated by those who made child development a scientific subject, both theory and practice. Perhaps he saw this as another example of the tendency to look outwards (at the child as an object of study and of treatment) and avoid looking within. It is all very well for people to hold ideals of training the personality of children: 'I can't help asking (wrote Jung) who it is that trains the personality'.[9] He would, I think, have made the same point in relation to the client-centred approach in social work (which hardly existed as a profession in his time), accepting it as a worthy ideal provided those who do the work attend to their own personality development. Both in education and social work we meet this same contrast between looking at the inward side or devising a technique that ensures we look only outwards, at children or clients as objects. It is hard indeed to accept the unconscious as real.

In an article in *The Listener,* John Macmurray[10] (a Quaker academic and moral philosopher) contrasted two categories of relationship. He called one Functional and the other Personal. These correspond to the two categories of psychology we have already considered, the objective and the subjective.

Functional relations exist for a practical purpose, as between colleagues or workmates in a factory or a service or an organization. Normally employees co-operate and contribute to the collective purposes. Adequate morale is essential for efficiency. The temperament, feelings and abilities of individuals tie-in with their responsibilities. Such emotions as optimism, zeal, self-esteem, ambition, enthusiasm and the ability to get on with others at work are all helpful. Strong personal and individual feelings, unrelated to the function of the organization, are a handicap. Good functionaries should not get involved at work in intense antagonisms, friendships or love affairs with their fellows. Their personal emotions should be kept within the limits of the organization's purpose and their own part in fulfilling it.

On the other hand, personal relations (said John Macmurray) are different in kind. They are independent of any particular function. If we warm to someone as a friend, purpose has nothing to do with it. Indeed, we shy away if we suspect a social acquaintance of being friendly towards us with some ulterior motive, whether financial, social, sexual or to obtain some advantage. The people we like and value and love mean much to us. They affect us emotionally. We warm to them for their own sake, for their intrinsic quality and worth, not in order to be used by them or to use them.

One may like someone as a friend but not as a colleague or vice versa. Or we may get on well at work and then find we become friends also. We can be rivals, competitors, antagonists at work but very good friends off duty. The two relationships are distinct even in ordinary daily life (unconnected with work). All kinds of difficulty can arise if they are confused. Too much friendly chat at the check-out or ticket-office is not popular and we should not bring a formal, professional attitude to those we meet at a party or on holiday. A works outing is not the same as a social gathering of friends.

We are here concerned with personal, not functional relationships (which are the province of scientific and industrial management in the interest of efficiency). Personal relations are emotional, not functional or formal. They are subjective not objective, human not scientific. They depend on value, not purpose, on meaning and not use. They are the province of friendship, of therapeutic (not laboratory or theoretical) psychology, of inner religion and spirituality, not technology. And they are at the heart of personal (not social) morality, based on goodwill not codes of practice, regulations, law or rules.

The quality of personal relations has always been the concern of religions, usually in the form of a moral code, an emphasis that has now become largely obsolete in terms of the individual, since a true spiritual orientation will provide its own morality. For Quakers this is illustrated by the conviction that there is 'that of God' in everyone. This is claimed as a conviction that rests not on dogma or theory but on experience. Such natural morality is not a cold duty or discipline imposed from without but a feeling, a response, akin to a child's spontaneous moral principle 'How would *you* like it?'. It rests on a natural fellow-feeling. But in spite of it, we have to face the plain fact of experience that we cannot always achieve such warmth and goodwill. This is another example of the psychological truth that our inner feelings are not within the control of the will.

This simple fact disturbs many earnest and sincere Christians. The Buddha likewise preached that 'karuna' (Sanscrit for active compassion) is the prime principle of moral behaviour. And that, too, is an emotion that arises spontaneously within us. Jung's insistence on the moral neutrality of our inner feelings which arise willy-nilly from the personal unconscious is sometimes disputed by Christians. They quote the saying of Jesus[11] that to look lustfully is equivalent to committing adultery in one's heart. Yet, on a different occasion, he dismayed his hearers by his tolerant attitude to the unfortunate woman taken 'in the very act'[12] (her lover apparently not being noticed by her accusers). We must not be delayed here by moral hairsplitting or casuistry but nevertheless may point out that his response to the public demand for her punishment silenced her accusers. How? Not by sentiment or an appeal to compassion but by drawing attention to the shadowside of their own rectitude, the insight that their righteous indignation sprang from their own unacknowledged lust. This response was a courageous and dangerous reply to their outraged righteousness. Were they too among those who afterwards cried 'Crucify him'?

An easy, natural morality is difficult to achieve in our hectic, bossy, aggressive and competitive way of life. One may get its savour from Taoism, a teaching that to Western minds seems mere laissez-faire, an abrogation of moral responsibility, a lack of discipline and manly vigour. So it is, but it discovered and proclaimed something very precious instead, a happy, flowing way along the path of Tao (the way things are).

The rigours of a Zen Buddhist training achieve something of the same kind. Perhaps the nearest Western equivalent is the green-fingered gardener who knows intuitively the way things like to grow and what they need; or the master craftsman, deft and relaxed, the expert nurse whose training has gone from her head to her hands, her manner, her voice, her presence, or the mother who knows the ways of her infant though she may have little knowledge of the theory of baby-care, or the soloist through whose hands music flows like a stream. The happiness of these wonderful people is catching. But for us, in the West and now, it is hard to understand that all this apparently effortless mastery has been achieved through a combination of training and love that can only be called religious in character and is now a natural grace. We so easily equate religion with keeping our noses to some moral grindstone, eternally vigilant against sin and temptation, never relaxed.

We tend to think morality (even love) comes from theology, bible study or charismatic conversion and sentimentality, instead of naturally from the heart. Some of us try to copy the relaxed Eastern ways and devices. But nature and spiritual tradition are not easily forced into a strange mould. God is not mocked, or deceived by drug-taking or inhaling, by deep breathing or strange postures or hypnotic chanting or such devices. One may be seduced into a spiritual dead-end by mystery and strangeness, but that is foolishness. 'People are incredibly eager (wrote Jung) to be rid of themselves, running after strange gods whenever occasion offers'.[13] What is needed is the will and the ability to get to the heart of another way to the spiritual life, 'to seek fresh light from whatever quarter it may come'.[14] Such light can only be found inwards, not by devices.

Feelings of warmth, kindness and goodwill arise, apparently spontaneously from the unconscious, towards some people but not to all. We do not make a conscious choice of whom we will like and help or dislike and avoid. It is decided for us by the unconscious (that 'queer fellow'), presumably on deep-laid criteria and early experiences and relationships. Strong and opposite feelings, likes and dislikes, affection and indifference, attraction and repulsion can emerge unexpectedly and suddenly. Sometimes, confusingly, such a pair of opposite feelings as any of those may emerge towards the same individual, to whom we may be compulsively attracted, much against our better judgment. Jung invites us to face these conflicts by realizing they are neither praiseworthy nor blameworthy but (as Alfred Adler constantly averred) feelings are a preparation for action, for behaviour. But what action we do take is a conscious, moral choice. Easy to say—hard to do. Why? Simply because the source of many of our strongest emotions lies obscure, in the shadow. Even their nature may be unrecognized by us. This issue is fundamental to moral freedom and therefore the concern of both psychology and religion.

Before the discoveries of the analysts, morals held supreme sway, with the conviction that we are always wholly responsible for our feelings and hence for our actions. But how can this be so since we are sometimes quite unaware what our feelings are, how they have arisen, and are simply carried away? There cannot be moral responsibility without freedom. Before the work of Freud and his collaborators this limitation was recognized only in the extreme instance of insanity (termed being 'not responsible') and in the legal system by the recognition of provocation, which means the acknowledgement that in certain circumstances the hypothetical 'normal person' would have acted the same way as the accused. Depth psychology has since then thrown much light on this necessary but indefinite fiction of normality and has still further shaken our earlier assumptions.

In the present context, we have veered in the opposite direction. Thanks to psychology, we tend to think that not only are emotions not our own responsibility but neither is the way we act on them. Some of the more dogmatic religious sects revert to the extreme position of total responsibility, other sects to the opposite pole in which there is no longer such a thing as immorality but only licence and sickness.

Many people incorrectly believe that analysts, psycho-therapists, counsellors, Child Guidance experts and psychiatrists have proved moral responsibility to be a chimera or at best a collective convenience for ensuring discipline. No wonder we are faced with collective social disorder and individual irresponsibility, violence, cruelty, crime and ever more divorces. Church teaching seems mostly hesitant and undecided on this. But it cannot be ignored, however difficult it is, because in actual living and working, responsibility rests ultimately not on dogma or rules but on feelings, on goodwill, and on response to the needs and sufferings of others and a sense of their intrinsic value as individuals. The conventional Quaker stance that there is 'that of God' but not that of evil in all people must be open to psychological questioning. It is not valid to see evil only as sickness, error, ignorance or the absence of good.

Anyone who disputes this challenging thought would do well to read Bruno Bettelheim's account of his experiences in a concentration camp[15] or Solzhenitsyn's short autobiographical novel.[16]

This complex problem of responsibility and the unconscious can, I suggest, be summed up as follows, which is an attempt to describe the present climate of general opinion or popular view.

First, although our temperament is inborn, our attitudes, values and spontaneous reactions have been absorbed in childhood.

Second, in early childhood our key experiences are in relation to our parents. If there is hate there, we absorb hate. If love is there, we learn it. And so on through the whole stock of feelings, attitudes and assumptions that our parents held. From being praised and punished we formed assessments of mother and father and of our own worth.

Third, as we developed, we became gradually aware of our own identity and began to use 'I'. We began to see ourselves as good or bad, lovable or unlovable, wanted or not wanted, useful or useless, these being not thoughts but feelings.

Fourth, from our parents we formed our own inner attitudes to food, to toilet training, to sex (so far as we could understand it), to the expression or suppression of emotion, ways of behaving and to the way parents treat each other.

Fifth, there were unavoidable conflicts. Our infantile or childish behaviour sometimes met unaccountable praise or blame because it conflicted with our parents' conscious (and particularly their unconscious) attitudes and values. We were thus unavoidably affected by whatever they felt most strongly, even when it conflicted with what they might profess.

Sixth, we tended to identify ourselves with the parent of the same sex if the relationship was a happy one or we rejected that image if it was unhappy. And we inevitably gained impressions of femaleness and maleness from the way we saw them.

Seventh, sometimes we were blamed and punished for things we could not help, wetting and dirtying, temper tantrums, crying. We were being moulded according to our parents' conscious ideals, values, ambitions and stereotypes and affected by their unconscious convictions.

Eighth, at puberty we began to rebel and entered a metamorphosis of physical (especially sexual) development, new idealisms, new rivalries and romantic idealisms, vocational uncertainty, an urge to break away from parental influence and assert a sense of independence. We presented something of a puzzle, even a threat, to them at a period of their own inner uncertainty as they entered middle age—their own metamorphosis.

All this (necessarily over-simplified) represents the general message we learnt from our upbringing, according to generally-accepted notions derived from psychology. It is very different from the earlier assumption that a child could (and should) be drilled and disciplined into learning and correct behaviour and right attitudes and acceptable emotions in the way we train animals, by reward, punishment, repetition and discipline (which, by the way, Freud called rationalized hatred).

In our present Western social context, concentration on the child rather than on those who bring him up has (as mentioned earlier) distorted the important question of relationship between parents and children. As I write these words, a tremendous publicity campaign has been launched against child abuse. Children are being encouraged to report ill-treatment by telephone on specially allocated lines. To whom? That is the question Jung would have asked and where he would have directed attention. Who are these kindly, sympathetic listeners entrusted with such a delicate and responsible relationship to children they do not know and have never even met? And what is the probable reaction of the offending parent?

I mention this as an instance of a best-intentioned attempt to resolve a most involved and delicate problem and deal with situations fraught with brutality and terrible suffering. After all the publicity, what? How can such cruelties be remedied by telephone or television, swamping the efforts of hard-pressed professional and experienced workers in their most delicate and personal, subjective and individual work? Quakers may like to consider, from this same point of view, the publicity given to victims of rape, exposing their dreadful experiences and traumas before a very large audience at the 1986 Yearly Meeting in Exeter (published in the Swarthmore lecture series[17]).

There is a popular belief that to publicise a problem is to solve it, that to arouse mass feelings of compassion, anger, outrage will somehow ensure a quick remedy to longstanding and deep-seated psychological problems. The first result is to exacerbate feelings of aggression and vengeance against those who are in desperate need of skilled treatment. Blame and outrage solve nothing. In any matter that depends primarily on raising money (for instance, following a famine, earthquake or other natural disaster), skilled mass publicity is triumphantly successful. But in matters that require personal understanding of a high order and need time-consuming therapeutic skill of great delicacy and insight, something very different is essential. Once more we face the confusion that arises from treating subjective, emotional problems by means that are effective for those that are functional, objective and impersonal. This error may even make matters worse. Heaven protect the child victims of brutal parents who discover their child has reported them to the BBC.

And how is all this connected with Quaker practice? Do we help one another to find a balance of inner and outer, conscious and unconscious, in our individual and our corporate life?

We have no substitute for confession to a priest nor is Meeting for Worship an appropriate occasion for it. Neither do we provide skilled therapy, which is sometimes compared and contrasted with religious confession. We are surely wise to leave such work to those who are trained to do it. Do we, then, neglect what Jung believed to be essential, namely the prime task of personal growth towards personal wholeness and integrating the mental (moral), the spiritual (inner religious) and the physical (material) sides of the personality?

Jung maintained that growth towards wholeness (which he termed individuation) should not be equated with therapy but is a natural process. Like other forms of growth and development, it is a lifelong task. He criticized those who pride themselves on 'staying young' when they are old or middle-aged, just as he criticized those who attempt to force the development of children. Here again we can learn from the Taoists. Jung saw therapy as the best available help when the natural process has become obstructed, much as one removes a stone that checks the growth of a plant. In a religious and psychological sense, Meeting for Worship provides this kind of support and help very effectively. To continue the analogy, if the plant itself is ailing, more expert help is required, as well as removing the stone. At its best, true Quaker ministry works in this way. A thought comes to us spontaneously out of the silence. We reflect on it and its appropriateness within the context of the meeting. Then we decide it is not helpful and keep quiet or we feel it has in it something that fits in. Then we find ourselves on our feet.

This is not free-association nor is it an unconsidered voicing of some sudden hunch. It is a balance between a thought that has bubbled up and reflection on its value in the meeting. Hence the essential pause after anyone has ministered, during which this balance is arrived at. As all Quakers know, an instant reply is out of place and disruptive.

Helpful ministry arises to some degree from personal experience but is not just an account of something interesting or moving. It has meaning for the one who speaks, has contributed something to personal development or understanding and has relevance to the corporate values of other members. Thus it is not confession though it may contain a call for help. It is not a submission to others of something for which their moral judgment is sought.

Thus the Quaker way of meeting can provide a safe, constructive, helpful and shared middle way between therapy and confession. What George Gorman called this 'amazing fact of Quaker worship'[18] combines inner and outer, freedom and convention, in an atmosphere pervaded by a sense of something or some entity greater than ourselves whose nature we corporately seek to understand and share. This entity in some compelling but mysterious way enshrines the supreme value towards which (or whom) we are inwardly directed. Within the limitations of our imperfections Meeting for Worship can offer an enlightening experience that combines psychological, moral and spiritual factors.

4 The Religious Attitude

An awareness of some entity greater than ourselves is, perhaps, the chief characteristic of a religious attitude to life. It is not belief or even faith, but certainty arising from experience. It gives one a meaning to life and a source of confidence, exhilaration and joy, in spite of circumstances. It is less of an intellectual or philosophical assessment of values than an inner calling. Paradoxically it may be both certain and vague—certain emotionally and yet vague in definition. It yields a sense of aim and direction.

In Jung's view, to develop a religious attitude to life is a natural process of growth towards wholeness and harmony, particularly typical of middle age. He found this challenge faced every one of all his middle-aged patients.[1] He added 'This of course has nothing to do with a particular creed or membership of a church'.[2] He believed, from his experience of hundreds of patients, that from the age of about thirty-five one's sphere of interest turns increasingly inwards. He regarded this reversal as a vital phase of personal development. In the first half of life our attention and energy have to be directed largely outwards, towards getting established among friends and colleagues, developing active abilities, strength and prowess and seeking the goal of our outward ambitions. Then around middle age there comes a time of asking what it is all for, a renewed and intensified interest in ideals, meanings and values that have had to lie more or less dormant and unformed since adolescence. This is a curious parallel to the old term for the menopause, 'involution'. It is a turning inwards not (as was formerly thought) of the uterus during the 'change of life', but of the psyche during middle age. The reversal of interest and of attention may be sudden or gradual, according to the extent to which the inner aspect of life has hitherto been unconscious. The discovery (or rediscovery) of inner concerns, interests and abilities during middle age is so common as to be normal. Perhaps

41

it is the basis of the saying that 'life begins at forty'. If we listen to the promptings from within (from the unconscious) we shall make new discoveries, develop new insight and relish a greater freedom from family cares and chores and from the pressure of ambition. We have a new freedom to make experiments.

Many visitors and attenders at our Sunday meetings are at this stage of life and find that conventional religion no longer answers their need (just as some leave us for a different denomination). Some find silent worship too much for them and do not return. Others feel at home and stay. Others remain as regular or occasional attenders. Some of these do not consider themselves orthodox Christians though their outlook is sympathetic to the Quaker way. Jung believed that the living spirit outgrows its earlier forms of expression and that 'measured against it, the names and forms that men have given it mean little enough'.[3] The same thought has often been expressed in a Quaker context, for instance, 'The ideas of God and man which have been held in the past must be re-expressed in the light of our own experience and further knowledge',[4]

Those people who reject a former faith do not necessarily abandon a religious attitude to life. Jung commented 'The individual's decision not to belong to a Church does not necessarily denote an anti-Christian attitude; it may mean exactly the reverse.'[5] Such attenders and visitors perhaps find, in the words of a scientist, 'that Quakerism in dispensing with creeds holds out a hand to the scientist. The scientific objection is not merely to particular creeds which assert in outworn phraseology beliefs which are either no longer held or no longer convey inspiration to life. The spirit of seeking which animates us refuses to regard any kind of creed as its goal. It would be a shock to come across a university where it was the practice to recite adherence to Newton's laws of motion, to Maxwell's equations and to the electro-magnetic theory of light'.[6] He went on a little later to affirm 'Rejection of creed is not inconsistent with being possessed by a living belief. We have no creed in science but we are not lukewarm in our beliefs. ... Religion for the conscientious seeker is not all a matter of doubt and self-questionings. There is a kind of sureness which is very different from cocksureness'.[7] Jung made it clear that his many observations about God should not be taken as a proof of God's existence. What he did claim is that we have within us an image of the Deity. Such an image is a fact of experience, not a logical proof. William James made much the same observation in the final lecture of his Gifford series: 'So long as we deal with the cosmic and the general, we deal only with the symbols of reality, but *as soon as we deal with private and personal phenomena as such, we deal with realities in the completest sense of the term,*'[8] (his italics).

I do not think all Quakers would be happy with this. Those of us who are used to earlier forms of expression of Quaker faith do not always take readily to a less rigid interpretation of what, for us, are immutable truths, even though not enshrined in a formal creed. We have to be true to the truth as we understand it, knowing that others on the same quest will sometimes understand it differently. This openness is welcomed by those who are natural seekers rather than faithful followers, whether they are inquiring visitors to our meetings or Quakers of long standing.

George Gorman described Quaker worship as 'an individual form of human activity, when we purposively put ourselves in the position of paying particular attention to those things in life which have the greatest meaning for us. In this sense worship is a sitting down in the presence of our values'.[9] Many people value this experience, with a feeling of release. Others do not want it. Perhaps it is too individual for them. They perhaps need the security of doctrine, of formally-accepted beliefs and regard religious worship as an occasion for confirming and repeating beliefs. In particular, some people do not wish to sit down in the presence of our values, that is, those held by the worshipping group, some of whom may not regard themselves as Christians. If values are to be expressed (they may think) then let them be the proven Christian values, so that we may be reminded of them and encouraged to live by them. The difficulty here is to decide what are Christian values. People speak of Christian charity and Christian forgiveness, for instance. But how are these different from plain charity or plain forgiveness? Christians cannot monopolise these or any other human virtues.

Quakers do not meet in worship only to share values. They claim to meet in the presence of God. This conviction stimulates the expectant emotional intensity characteristic of a gathered meeting, even though each person present has an individual understanding of what is meant by the word God. To some God is indeed present and we can relate to him as to a personality. To these people Meeting for Worship is assembling in God's presence. Arthur Eddington supported this view of God in personal terms: 'We have to build the spiritual world out of symbols taken from our own personality, as we build the scientific world out of the symbols of the mathematician. I think therefore we are not wrong in embodying the significance of the spiritual world to ourselves in the feeling of a personal relationship, for our whole approach to it is bound up with those aspects of consciousness in which personality is centred'.[10]

Many Quakers and attenders share this view. But for some it is not real. They cannot visualise God in man's likeness nor bring themselves to think of God as male. Others think of God in terms of spiritual energy, others as the supreme value, others again as love, beauty and goodness or as the creator. Such differences did not concern Jung. In his view, we should accept ultimate things as we experience them and if they help us towards completeness and a better life then, he said. 'You may safely say "This was the grace of God". No proof of any superior truth is implied by this'.[11] He maintained that we can understand religious matters only through personal experience. The same is true even of faith: 'The seat of faith is not consciousness but religious experience'.[12] Assertions of faith or of metaphysics, in his view, can be neither proved nor disproved. The assertions themselves, however, are facts that have to be taken into account. They are real though they may not be true in any literal sense and they are often powerful for good or for evil.

In a section of his Swarthmore lecture headed 'The Rejection of Religion', George Gorman describes how he tried to rid himself of the concept of God but could not quite succeed, possibly because of his religious upbringing. He then came across Quakers and found, to his surprise, that 'For them religious experience didn't look much like what I thought to be religious at all'.[13] He found that although they had 'a strong sense of the reality of God, Quakers nevertheless emphasized that the starting point of religious experience is always to be found in ordinary everyday experience'[14] and that they did not draw a sharp line between sacred and secular. After discussion with many of them and much reading of the literature, especially *Christian Faith and Practice,* he found that in spite of differences he could recognize 'a continuous search for truth, life, love, God, call it what you will, in and through the everyday experiences of life itself'.[15] This suggested to him that their religious faith arises out of daily experience 'by a process of looking for signals of transcendence'.[16]

This brings us to two alternative ways of building faith: letting it grow out of one's personal experience of living or, on the contrary, first finding faith and then interpreting experience accordingly. The latter has long been a conventional Christian way, Church leaders insisting that one must have faith, then everything else will follow. Jung objected that faith cannot be had to order. Moreover, there seems, in this approach, to be a risk that we find in experience what we are looking for (a common pitfall). Such looking is often unconscious and is then all the more powerful. Hence the dramatic conversion of someone who has been a militant atheist or humanist or enemy of the Church, the classic instance being the conversion of Saul of Tarsus. If George Gorman's conclusion is correct, this distinction marks off the Quaker way from that of most other Christian Churches, who rely on the primacy of faith. Perhaps the chicken-and-egg quality is not all that important. Both approaches depend on a conviction expressed by Francis H. Knight as being 'in touch with something or someone beyond myself'.[17] The question then becomes whether I must get in touch with it or will it get in touch with me. Is a religious attitude to life inborn or acquired, sought deliberately or does it emerge from the unconscious?

We will first consider the search or quest. This is an ancient tradition and appears often in mystical and poetic writings. In symbolic form it was the basic theme of the legendary Grail Quest. Thus John Matthews, introducing his book on this topic, wrote 'No matter what form the quest took, the objective remained the same: a spiritual goal representing inner wholeness, union with the divine, self-fulfilment'.[18] Even today, the Arthurian legends have their hold over us and Glastonbury still keeps something of its magic. For Jung, the devoted absorption of medieval alchemists, at first sight such ridiculous dabbling in non-chemistry by later standards, was an immensely and compulsively powerful symbolic search for the same union with the divine. So was the cult of the rose garden, so skilfully and sensitively described by Eithne Wilkins.[19]

What did George Gorman mean by 'signals of transcendence'? I think he was referring to the spiritual meaning that can be found in daily life and which provides evidence that we can in some measure unite with what he called 'truth, life, love, God, call it what you will'.[20] Like John Matthews, Jung would I think have regarded this experience as 'inner wholeness, union with the divine, self-fulfilment'.[21]

Some Quakers do not find this idea of a search quite apt. Ole Olden, for instance, preferred 'explore' to 'seek', commenting 'We do not seek the Atlantic, we explore it. The whole field of religious experience has to be explored, and has to be described in a language understandable to modern men and women'.[22] Arthur Eddington pointed out that seeking implies finding which, he said, is what we are hoping for. He continued 'Yet how transitory it proves. The finding of one generation will not serve for the next'.[23] Nevertheless, in spite of this, he adds 'You will understand the true spirit neither of science nor of religion unless seeking is placed in the forefront'.[24] H. G. Wood wrote 'In this life of the spirit we may all start as seekers, but happy are we if we become explorers'.[25] And, after all, that is what happened with the alchemists and the grail seekers.

The alternative view is that we are not seekers but are sought. Francis Thompson's famous poem 'The Hound of Heaven' is a vivid expression of this. It is perhaps more in accord with the way most Quakers approach Meeting for Worship. This was put clearly by Rufus M. Jones. He explained that we find silence to be one of the best preparations for communion with God 'and for the reception of inspiration and guidance ... The actual meeting of man with God and God with man is the very crown and culmination of what we can do with our human life'.[26] Are Quakers, then, both active seekers and passive receivers in a spiritual sense? Or do we tend to start active and become receptive?

I believe the general tenor of Jung's teaching on this is clear: that we can prepare ourselves to accept what may be offered to us through the unconscious. But we cannot find and possess it by actively searching. Ralph Hetherington's Swarthmore lecture dealt with this distinction in connection with the work of Abraham H. Maslow. Speaking of the way we experience other people and things, he said 'We can see them either in terms of our own needs and as potential satisfiers of those needs; or we can see them ... in and for themselves, undistorted by any self-centred need or desire'.[27] Following Maslow, he distinguished these alternatives by seeing the former as associated with 'deficiency needs' and the other as associated with 'growth motives'. This resembles John Macmurray's[28] distinction between functional relationships and personal relationships based on intrinsic value—that is to say on acceptance or love. We may, I suggest, make a similar distinction in our attitude to God and to the unconscious, either seeking help for ourselves or accepting a relationship for its intrinsic value, as in the presence of someone we love. Some religious teachers distinguish between a prayer of petition and a prayer of adoration.

Jung would have us see the unconscious as a friend, but

one who has no moral sense. It will sometimes present us with what our rational mind must reject on moral grounds. At other times it will present us with what is valuable and creative. This gives us a say in how we act. If, on the contrary, we are unable to accept the unconscious we remain ignorant of what it is trying to convey to us. Then it will find its own way to get a hearing and will influence us unawares in some negative mood or unexplained hostility which our moral judgment is powerless to direct. George Gorman was aware of this. Referring to centring down at Meeting for Worship, he wrote 'While the exercise of centring down is not mere introspection, it does mean the willingness to allow ourselves to be vulnerable and exposed to the darkness as well as to the light within. For none of us is without the shadow side to our lives, which we skilfully repress into the unconscious'.[29] This is surely an unusual view for a Quaker to hold. (The last few words of the quotation may suggest that we deliberately repress unacceptable urges, but that is not so. Repression happens, it is not voluntary. We cannot make something unconscious by an act of will nor prevent it emerging into consciousness of its own accord.)

This is an issue of great importance in progress towards wholeness, as well as to the orderly and friendly conduct of life and the quality of our relationships. We may consciously and sincerely endorse the importance of accepting people as they are (that is to say, loving our neighbour) but what if hostility or envy bubbles up inside us and spoils it? We can direct our inner urges only to the extent that they are conscious.

We come now to the question whether in Meeting for Worship we have direct experience of God. Quakers speak of the Light of Christ as impeccable and usually regard worship as opening ourselves to its influence and to waiting in the presence of God, that is to say, of the all-loving Creator and source of all that is good in the world. Yet George Gorman quotes Alistair Kee: 'There is no direct experience of God, only experiences which are interpreted in a religious manner'.[30] George Gorman says that he was particularly drawn to that statement 'as to my mind it catches succinctly the essential approach made by Quakers, even though at first glance it appears to challenge them to modify their long-held claim that in their life and worship they have direct and immediate experience of God. On reflection this will be seen to be human experience which Quakers have felt obliged to interpret in a religious manner'.[31]

This quotation brings us close to the position taken by Jung. In his view 'We cannot tell whether God and the unconscious are two different entities. Both are borderline concepts for transcendental contents'.[32] Later in the same passage he wrote 'The religious need longs for wholeness, and therefore lays hold of the images of wholeness offered by the unconscious'.[33]

These reflections on the religious attitude in our present context give a more sophisticated picture than the simple attitude of the early Quakers. There are those who would feel happier if we could maintain that early simplicity. But it seems the fate of our time that we have to re-think and re-experience many of these issues in the light of a more detailed understanding of our human psyche.

In the wider context of the Churches generally and the general attitude towards religion in its inner manifestations, we meet many uncertainties. For instance, we are surrounded by people who band together into enthusiastic partisan movements and causes that in some ways resemble religions. Some of these are political, many are motivated by genuine and intense concern for justice and tolerance, fair treatment for minorities, animals, or what is now called the environment (formerly called nature), for beauty or for mystical experience or for artistic expression. The partisan and specialized nature of the concerns and the single-minded zeal with which they are usually imbued distinguish them from religion in the spiritual sense. They thrive on protest and propaganda, on collective zeal illustrated by slogans and gestures, marches, demonstrations, and dependence on publicity in our frenzied media-dominated way of life.

These seem a far cry from the individual-orientation of

Quaker practice and of psychotherapy and it would be unwise to under-estimate the explosive energy that motivates them collectively. But they are not in the same category as those aspects of religion that spring from the depths of the individual unconscious in the presence of some supreme value. They resemble strongly evangelistic and fundamentalist sects that are essentially collective rather than individual. Jung would not, I believe, have regarded these partisan and specialized militant campaigns as religions, since they are not characterized by any true acceptance of the divine. 'I want to make clear (wrote Jung) that by the term "religion" I do not mean a creed'.[34] In his view, the essential is not a formal statement of belief but personal experience of the numinosum. In his last book, Jung defined this term as 'Rudolph Otto's term (in his *Idea of the Holy*) for the inexpressible, mysterious, terrifying, directly experienced and pertaining only to the divinity'.[35] In Jung's view inner, spiritual and subjective experience of the divine (powerful enough to modify consciousness) is the essential character of religion.

Among the various sects, partisan 'causes', cults and movements that surround us now, there are two divisions that we need to consider here. The first is between the individual approach and the collective, the second between the spiritual and secular. The word 'numinosum' (in the quotation just given) helps to make these distinctions clear. The numinous is an intensely personal, private and mysterious category, virtually indescribable. In a social atmosphere dominated by commercial, material and collective values, it is an object of distrust and disbelief. In primitive cultures it takes collective rather than individual forms in taboos and totems, cults and superstitions and the acceptance of the power of gods, spirits, charms and ritual. In our society all such things are suspect. Those who are subject to superstition are regarded as odd, cranky and living in a world of their own and perhaps mad or at least 'touched'.

In spite of this suspicion, gropings after the numinous are quite common today, in new forms of mythology, in artistic experiment, black magic, exorcism, devil worship, astrology and occult practices, science fiction, imaginary cultures and societies, invasions from other worlds, flying saucers, extra-sensory perception and so forth. Some of the older forms lose their hold, such as fortune-telling, crystal-gazing, palmistry, phrenology. They are replaced by new kinds of magic, mystery and pseudo-science. Today, talk of peak experience is commonplace, whether sought through drugs, yoga, meditative practices or through works of art, particularly music.

In 1975 Ralph Hetherington (a distinguished Quaker clinical psychologist) delivered the Swarthmore lecture already referred to. In it, he gave a psychological account of the sudden incursion into awareness of the exalted ecstasy of the peak experience. It would be impertinent of me to attempt to summarize his masterly and balanced account, all of which is relevant to the topic we are considering. There are, however, some points that are of particular concern here. For instance, are the experiences he describes authentically numinous, in Rudolf Otto's sense? Are they spiritual or secular or physical in origin, or perhaps a mixture of these? How are they related to the Quaker experience of the Inner Light? Are they truly religious? Are they connected with artistic or scientific creative flashes of insight so comprehensively explained in Arthur Koestler's book *The Act of Creation*?[36] And what bearing, if any, has Jung's understanding of the unconscious on these experiences?

So far as individuals are concerned, the whole area of the numinous comprises both the ridiculous and the sublime, the spiritual and the phoney, the holy and the charlatan, the genuine and the bogus. To many it seems reasonable to see this strange ferment as arising from the failure of conventional and traditional religion to meet the spiritual needs of the majority as it formerly did before science and rationality destroyed belief in dogma. The practical, material, objective part of us dismisses cranky groups and their activities as nothing but examples of irrational phantasy and human credulity (which some of them are) and unreal (which they are not). The spiritual part of us asks, with Jung, 'What great thing was not at first phantasy?'[37]

We must acknowledge that the great and lasting achievements of mankind and of civilization (in the sense given by Kenneth Clark[38]) stem from the spiritual part of life, not the practical and logical, as do the deepest and most precious feelings of one person for another. To John Macmurray's helpful distinction between functional and personal relationships, we should perhaps add a third, namely spiritual. This would give to some personal relationships a more extensive meaning than he did. It would recognize a special kind of potential value, perhaps included in Martin Buber's famous I-Thou relationships, characterized not only by mutual friendliness and respect but also a numinous quality. Conventional Christians recognize this as arising from the fatherhood of God; for most Quakers, I think it arises from 'that of God' in every person. In Jung's terminology it arises from that which is 'pertaining only to the deity'.[39]

In his book *True Resurrection*, Harry Williams (a member of the Mirfield Community of the Resurrection and former Dean of Trinity College, Cambridge) links people, places and works of art as sharing potential unity with us.[40] They mysteriously offer to share their being with us and we experience them as beyond explanation, adequate description or definition—in short, mysterious. We can share with them but not possess them in their unique reality. Such communion, he said, 'is identical with love'.[41] This must sound far-fetched to objective, practical minds but it would have been commonplace to the Romantics. And I fear such talk would have raised Quakerly eyebrows among our puritanical predecessors, and may do so today among faithful followers of the old way. But for explorers of any denomination or any religion it represents a recognizable part of life and has the immediate and unequivocal reality of a peak experience, that is to say, of the numinous, the divine. Ralph Hetherington did not go so far as this but included people, places and works of art among his examples of such experiences. Moreover, he wisely commented, near the end of his lecture, that 'the world of being has to inform and inspire the world of becoming'.[42]

This should reassure those of us who are concerned that our puritan feet should remain on the ground, even if our head (psyche) sometimes strays into cloudland (the cloud of unknowing—yes, but also of communion with the divine). George Gorman too did not go so far as Harry Williams. He stopped short at the 'gateway of transcendence',[43] almost shyly declining to enlarge on what Quakers mean by the Holy Spirit. Considering how readily one may be carried away on a wave of fringe occultism, perhaps the sober caution of Quakers towards transcendence is wise, if unadventurous. Danger lies, though, not in transcendence or the numinous but in irresponsible, unworldly absorption or, much worse, in psychic epidemics of collective fanaticism and mass hysteria. The worst examples of these may be recognized by aggressive, power-seeking zeal and a conviction that those who disagree are enemies to be vilified, misrepresented or attacked. Even among Quakers, the heady joy of collective irrationality for a good cause and wanting everyone to think as we do, is sometimes a temptation.

'Only the man [i.e. person] who can consciously assent to the power of the inner voice becomes a personality'[44] wrote Jung and went on to say that this does not mean we should succumb to it. Once again we are reminded that the inner voice is amoral. But according to Jung, it should not (indeed must not) be disregarded because of that. Its messages challenge our moral sense, so that we can rightly direct its life-giving energy. 'The inner voice is the voice of a fuller life, of a wider, more comprehensive consciousness', said Jung and continued that the unconscious may whisper 'something negative, if not actually evil'[45] and that it is both tempting and convincing. Our task is to accept it without guilt or hostility, for it is a bringer of healing and illumination. 'The highest and the lowest, the best and the vilest, the truest and the most deceptive things are often blended together in the inner voice.'[46] It is the tension between these opposites that gives the inner voice its characteristic energy.

An extension of this view brings us to the importance Jung attributed to personal vocation. One who listens to the inner voice is 'called'. It is (this calling) 'an irrational factor that destines a man [person] to emancipate himself from the herd and from its well-worn paths. True personality is always a vocation and puts its trust in God.'[47] In Quaker literature we read of the inner light rather than voice and therefore do not hear much about vocation. The difference is one of metaphor rather than substance; there is the same sense of inner direction and obedience, whether we think of it in terms of a voice that calls and sends us or of a light that shows us the way and our own particular path along it. But what is the source? Quakers have testified to the light of Christ that shines in our hearts. For Jung, the voice that summons and directs us is in the unconscious, where God speaks. The problem for religious people is to come to terms with the voice of evil, of temptation, of a darkness that is more potent than the mere absence of light and the personal shadow that we wish to escape from.

According to Quaker thought, the inner light is not the same as conscience, which is simply that which sees the light. 'The light that shines into man's heart is not of man, and must ever be distinguished from both the conscience which it enlightens, and from the natural faculty of reason ... As the eye is to the body, so is conscience to our inner nature, the organ by which we see'.[48] This inner light is the divine effluence, the will of God, the light of Christ. 'The inner light does not lead men to do that which is right in their own eyes, but that which is right in God's eyes'.[49]

What, then, in Quaker thinking is the origin of peak experiences, that ecstasy that comes to us as a 'grace', from human relationships, places, works of art? Today the puritanical stance of the early Quakers has been relaxed. Ormerod Greenwood's Swarthmore lecture of 1978[50] was as much a milestone in Quaker thinking about the arts as was Ralph Hetherington's (three years earlier) about the psychology of spirituality. Both are remarkable for the depth of their understanding and width of sympathy and have done much to free us from puritan mistrust of inner feeling. Ormerod Greenwood was impressed by a remark made by Damaris Parker-Rhodes in her Swarthmore lecture the previous year:[51] 'Many religious people never come to possess their inner selves, and they use their form of worship as a vaccination to keep them safe from living experience'.[52] Perhaps it was left for the wonderful Gerard Hoffnung to point our laughing way to yet another grace by which we learn to behold ever more of the light— namely, humour—and so, in spite of all, to 'walk cheerfully over the world'.[53]

This, then, must end our brief survey of the context in which Quaker thought and Jung's teaching converge at a time of religious uncertainty, spiritual exploration and mistrust of authority, a time in which the autonomy of inner conviction is breaking free from convention: an exciting time for those who can face the glare of 'new light from whatever quarter it may come'.[54]

PART TWO

Challenge

5 Belief and Disbelief: Faith and Doubt

In 1984 Don Cupitt (a philosopher and theologian, Dean of Emmanuel College, Cambridge) published *The Sea of Faith*, based on his television series for the BBC. In it he wrote of 'religion-shock', an equivalent of culture-shock. He explained, 'Religion-shock occurs when someone who is a strong believer in his own faith confronts, without evasion and without being able to explain it away, the reality of an entirely different form of faith, and faces the consequent challenge to his own deepest assumptions'.[1]

Today it is difficult for any religious believer to avoid being challenged by strong believers of another religion or a different denomination. There is also the challenge from the indifference or disbelief of sceptics and non-believers and devotees of secular ideology. These rivalries are mutual: each provokes the other, intentionally or unconsciously, regardless of which is in the majority. Our modern freedom to decide for oneself what to believe is balanced by the discomfort of such pressures or clashes, which are sometimes severely hostile.

In some respects, Jung's teaching has to be included among possible causes of religion-shock for Quakers. Inevitably, the stronger our beliefs the more disturbing the challenge will be (though the reverse is sometimes claimed). One wonders whether those who advised us to 'be ready at all times to receive fresh light'[2] and to 'approach new theories with discernment'[3] realized quite how much that advice would cost us a generation later.

By 'deepest assumptions' I think Don Cupitt meant the highly individual and personal network of ideas, values, feelings and thoughts which together make up our attitude to life and the meaning we give to life and find in life. It is not always religious: devotion to Fascism, Marxism or Communism (and the like) certainly involves a person's deepest assumptions. But Quaker assumptions are, of course, religious by definition, for they include acknowledgment of a divine entity.

Jung regarded a religious attitude as a natural development of the psyche, not peculiar to cultured, secure or good-living people or to members of any particular religious organization or indeed of any particular religious faith. 'The religious impulse (he wrote) rests on an instinctive basis . . . You can take away a man's gods, but only to give him others in return.'[4] Our human consciousness is such that we cannot avoid awareness of good and evil, birth and death, beauty, joy, ecstasy and suffering, love and hate, aggression and meekness. We are confronted by mystery (for all our technical mastery) and we are inwardly driven to respond to it, to try to understand it, to explain, to accept, to find a meaning to our predicament and in our experience.

There is nothing narrowly psychological about this need. It has always accompanied human consciousness, even in the remote past. The most critical mystery for a Christian is the existence and origin of evil in a world created, or supposedly created, by an all-loving and all-powerful God—a persistent source of doubt in spite of all the contributions of scholars, theologians and authorities. It is hard indeed to explain or justify or tolerate the dreadful weight of human suffering, the hideous proliferation of evil. Jung questioned the tendency to foist evil onto the devil or to see it wholly outside ourselves, individually and collectively. 'For all our progress . . . monstrous engines of destruction have been invented which could easily exterminate the human race.'[5]

Such developments have come from the human psyche, in his view, not from a fallen angel. He noted that in prehistoric times human beings apparently felt the reality of a 'primordial divine being'.[6] In the first century of our era, he observed, Clement of Rome (third in succession to Peter as bishop) taught that God rules the world with a right hand and a left hand, the right being Christ, the left Satan. 'All his life (wrote Anthony Storr) Jung wrestled with the problem of the origin of evil'.[7] He explained 'The conventional Christian view of God is dualistic, in that God is entirely good (the doctrine of the Summun Bonum) while evil is contained in Satan'.[8] Jung points out that an earlier Christian belief was monotheistic. That is to say that the concept of God embraced both good and evil.

When we are baffled by these mysteries, belief comes to our rescue, especially if it is a belief that we can share. We mostly think our beliefs are rational, that after proper consideration we have made a conscious choice. Yet, who is reasoned out of a conviction? Or into one? 'He proved his point (we may say) but did not convince me' or 'I was utterly convinced in spite of all the reasons to the contrary' or 'All I can say is that it is my belief. That is all there is to it, say what you like.' Beliefs arise mainly from the unconscious (personal or collective). This gives them their peculiar tense quality. Belief is a specially sensitive area of the psyche. We are elated by whatever confirms a belief and made anxious by whatever questions or denies it. Most normal people pride themselves on the strength with which they are prepared to defend or assert what they believe. We cannot help but venerate those who have suffered for their beliefs, even when we do not share them.

What, then, are the principal beliefs and strongest assumptions of the ardent Christian believer? To try to answer this at once confronts us with the dual quality of belief, that it is both intellectual and emotional, both conscious in part and unconscious in part. Even if we are lukewarm in our beliefs we prefer to leave them undisturbed rather than put them into words. But there are also some who are impelled to voice what they believe, as though to provoke or challenge disagreement. Sometimes they protest too much. Evangelical zeal suggests not confidence but anxiety. There are yet other believers whose way is to purge emotion out of any discussion and treat belief as though it were wholly rational and intellectual.

Jung was not concerned with theological or philosophical answers to questions of belief, though he was much concerned with the way men and women face the mysteries of our human lot and the even greater mystery of our personal vocation, our call to become what we have in us to become, the internal challenge to grow towards wholeness. For him, as for Quakers, detailed discussion and argument of dogma, doctrine and belief screens us from the vital need to see the path before us and to progress along it. Theories, doctrines and academic study can shelter us from moral uncertainty and the anxiety of doubt; that is to say, from responsibility.

Jung wrote of 'the precious gift of doubt'.[9] That is a challenging phrase to a conventional Christian believer. It has generally been regarded as sinful to doubt any of the fundamentals of the faith. Indeed, to deny the doctrine of 'the real presence' in the sacrament was the ultimate heresy for which many were burnt at the stake, at the instigation of men utterly convinced that they were fulfilling God's will and the mission of Jesus. Our Quaker predecessors suffered persecution for heresy by fellow Christians. Even today, men, women and children are killed in the violence of sectarian rivalry in the same religion of love. Surely no one can regard the workings of the collective unconscious as unimportant or unreal when it has such results. It bursts forth, as it has always been liable to do, in religious fanaticism or political and national extremism with all the savagery and violence of a psychic epidemic, in defiance of all reason, compassion and goodwill.

'Dogma and fanaticism (wrote Jung) are always compensations for hidden doubt. Religious persecutions take place only where heresy is a menace'.[10] This applies not only collectively (in all forms of fanaticism) but within every individual fanatic, no matter how good he believes his cause to be. 'With me (said Robert Browning's bishop) faith means perpetual unbelief kept quiet'.[11] He was aware of the pressure of unbelief (which most fanatics are not) and took the conventional Christian way to deal with it by relying on faith. But faith, like belief, cannot be produced to order. Those who try to smother doubt by faith are still at risk. The unconscious cannot be forced by act of will. Belief and faith are not adequate for, (wrote Jung) 'wherever faith prevails, there doubt is always lurking.'[12] And yet, how often are religious doubters told they should have more faith. 'Where there is will-power, there is also won't-power' said Richard Hull (Jung's official translator).[13] According to Jung 'The man who is morally and spiritually more highly developed no longer wishes to follow a faith or a rigid dogma. He wants to understand'.[14] And elsewhere 'certainties can arise only through doubt and results through experiment'.[15]

Some visitors and attenders who sample Quaker Meeting for Worship have had a conventional and sincere upbringing and have been taught from childhood that doubt of religious doctrines is wrong and must be cured by faith. Others have had their doubts smothered by evangelical pressure and have been indoctrinated with ready-made beliefs, backed by the zeal of those who proclaim them, regarding themselves perhaps as missionaries. That is another way by which unbelief within may be kept quiet though not resolved. But, as Jung pointed out, 'Belief is no adequate substitute for inner experience'.[16]

It may be that such seekers hear in Meeting something that speaks to their condition, some sharing of religious insight. The anxiety of having to face inner doubt is wonderfully allayed by a silent meeting, though at first it may seem challenging, since it allows doubt to surface. But there is no pressure to escape from the challenge by talking or activity, no urgency to reply 'true' or 'untrue'. Even if there is no verbal ministry, the visitor may be greatly helped by the atmosphere of relaxed expectancy instead of discussion, argument, advice or assertion. It is as though doubts are acceptable, whether voiced or not. There is no feeling of judgment or criticism.

A simple example may serve to illustrate this. Suppose a visitor has from early childhood been taught to accept the resurrection of Jesus as a literal fact in the firm belief, as Hans Küng expressed it, that 'Easter is the origin and goal of faith'.[17] Suppose, too, that any hint of doubt or query has been met with disapproval and rejection, and belief imbued with the majesty of revealed dogma and demanded as a Christian's first duty. Yet no intelligent and educated adult can possibly believe that life can return to the dead. During the Meeting it may well be that there is no ministry that has direct bearing on this dilemma of belief. Nevertheless, from the silence or from ministry the visitor may begin to sense that there is another way of confronting it that does not demand an intellectual or verbal answer to a factual question, does not demand believing what is inherently impossible, that the pressure is unreal and unnecessary. Hans Küng himself (a Catholic theologian) followed those words of his (just quoted) by adding that the doctrine 'should not be turned into a law of faith'.[18] Jung stated that if the resurrection of Christ is understood symbolically, 'it is capable of various interpretations that do not conflict with knowledge and do not impair the meaning of the statement'.[19]

We pay a heavy toll for the Western over-emphasis on literal truth and the accompanying blindness to spiritual, symbolic and poetic truth that lies dormant within. The visitor may sense that there is another way of confronting doubt, not head-on as demanding a decision but as alerting us to its inner, spiritual meaning which, given the chance and freedom from pressure, may in time emerge from within, as sometimes happens when a poem eventually reveals the inner meaning that was hidden from us. (Harry Williams's book *True Resurrection* is particularly helpful on this whole matter.)

It is not, of course, only visitors and attenders who have doubts of such intensity and not much opportunity of resolving them, nor is it the case that every Meeting will be helpful to doubters in the way just indicated. The fifth chapter of George Gorman's Swarthmore lecture[20] gives a most helpful account of ways ministry may sometimes be unhelpful. There is one more way to be added because of its relevance in this present context. Perhaps one should call it one-sided affirmation, that is to say an affirmation of what are taken to be general Quaker beliefs, often somewhat healthy-minded in character. If based on experience this kind of ministry can be fresh and exhilarating since it echoes what we share and corporately believe. If it is not based on some new experience and is only a restatement of routine beliefs it adds nothing to the Meeting and is disheartening to those who are facing uncertainty or disbelief. This is the opposite of what is intended perhaps, since it is easy to think that a happy restatement of mutual belief and shared faith will encourage everyone. It is a kind of anodyne ministry, giving one a happy feeling that may be discouraging to anyone who needs help: it does not remotely speak to their condition. I referred to it as one-sided because it does not take account of its opposite but ignores it. Therefore it lacks vitality and falls flat.

This type of ministry is apt to arise when the belief behind it is lukewarm and is not associated with inner experience. This is a risk that is not easily dealt with. It was expressed with startling clarity in Leo Tolstoy's last (and supremely religious) novel, *Resurrection*, which incidentally incurred the anger of the religious hierarchy. He describes a religious service in the prison chapel. The author says of the officiating chaplain: 'He did not believe that the bread became flesh, or that it was good for the soul to pronounce a great number of words, or that he had really devoured a bit of God—no one could believe that— but he believed that one ought to believe it'.[21] This stark extract highlights a critical distinction, between beliefs that are accepted uncritically and without thought and those that have arisen as a spontaneous response from the deepest part of us (that is, from the unconscious), an echo in the heart so to speak, and then have been subjected to our careful and discriminating thought and perhaps also shared with others. That is how a firm belief is established and how accepted beliefs may be modified, amplified or even subsequently discarded. In Hans Küng's phrase, a belief is not 'a law of faith'.[22]

We now turn to the connection between belief and faith. Both of them comprise thinking and feeling and also both reason and emotion. Beliefs are, as it were, on approval, tentatively held. They may be modified by experience and later knowledge.

Faith is more complex. It is made up of feelings and beliefs, consciously and unconsciously, and gradually emerges as the network referred to earlier and constitutes the meaning we give to life. Faith often rests on strong, unconscious feelings and then we speak of conviction. It also has a basis of trust which inspires our loyalty and our ideals. Doubt of our faith is more painful than doubt of a particular belief.

When beliefs are integrated into one's faith they demand practical expression. In the words of the Austrian philosopher Ludwig Wittgenstein 'It strikes me that a religious belief could only be something like a passionate commitment to a system of reference. Hence, although it's belief, it's really a way of living, or a way of assessing life'.[23] Hans Küng was even more explicit on the same point: 'The ultimate criterion of a person's Christian spirit is not theory but practice: not how he thinks of teachings, dogmas, interpretations, but how he acts in ordinary life'.[24]

Faith, then, is a fusion of beliefs and committed action, action that has life in it and is not just a routine performance of duty or something done for advantage or amusement. It prompts us with that sense of vocation we considered earlier. The hallmark of faith is the confident energy it yields, not over-zealous but strangely untiring. Faith is expressed outwardly and also inwardly. When outlining some views of Kirkegaard, Don Cupitt wrote 'Religious teachings provide the itinerary; they show the course of the Path . . . Understood spiritually they become means to inner liberation. God becomes our saviour in so far as religious doctrines no longer constrain us externally but inspire and guide us inwardly'.[25]

These views in no way contradict Jung's. They confirm the Quaker insight that religion is not only an inward concern: we have practical obligations to fulfil and jobs to tackle. Our inner faith inspires and stimulates us to act as well us sometimes yielding a sense of glory or some peak experience. In John W. Harvey's Swarthmore lecture *The Salt and the Leaven* (1947) he explained that the value of action ('even humble, menial and manual action') is 'not merely as means to express a belief or conviction, but in order to confirm, even to create our faith in its validity. Not "Bring your belief to the proof of action, testify to it by practising it" but "Bring your half-belief into the power-

house of co-action that it may become full belief, creative
and compelling"'.[26] Well, this is strong stuff and maybe not
all of us would go quite so far as to maintain that faith can
arise out of action or that 'co-action' can turn half-belief
into full belief. But this is only a difference of emphasis. It
is a well-established Quaker view that action and faith
should be linked. No one quite approves of admirable
beliefs and strong faith that are not expressed in action or
are contradicted by behaviour. The official report of the
Friends World Conference of 1952 stated 'We claim to be a
movement, not a sect'.[27] A movement has a practical aim
and has stimulus: a sect is a sub-group dedicated to a
special system of belief.

So, then, our Quaker faith is threefold: it is expressed in
belief, action and spirituality. Some of us give precedence
to one of these, some to another. Our inner needs and the
demands of our situation may from time to time necessi-
tate a change of priority, for faith is no rigid system but a
working and harmonious trio. Some of us may now and
then get disquieted if we think our own Meeting or our
society is getting the priority wrong but 'Dependence on
the Holy spirit will lead us into unity'.[28] Jung challenges us
to take into account what the inner voice is trying to tell us,
what the inner light can reveal to us if we know how to
look. The interdependence of belief and action is more
familiar to most of us than is spirituality.
    Our faith—anyone's faith—is difficult to put into words
and is more belief than action. Spirituality is the specifically religious part of the trio and gives life and inspiration
to it. The puritan tradition concentrated on behaviour and
doctrine at the expense of spirituality which it tended to
distrust. Don Cupitt wrote: 'Until about 1700 or so the free
play of fantasy was regarded as dangerous and Christians
prayed to be protected from it . . . They thought they were
combating Satan, but as we now see it, they were in fact
fighting only against their own creativity'.[29] Some of us, I
think, would put that date a good deal later.
    The free play of phantasy is perhaps the most easily
recognized expression of unconscious thoughts, feelings

and ideas through the imagination. Some of us still find difficulty in trusting anything so unpredictable. Yet (wrote Jung) 'all creative work comes from imagination and phantasy . . . every creative individual . . . owes all that is greatest in his life to phantasy. The dynamic principle of phantasy is play'.[30] Play? What, one wonders, would our puritanical Quaker forefathers say to this? Yet, as George Bernard Shaw's Saint Joan told her examiner, the imagination 'is how the messages of God come to us'.[31] Of course, we have to do our best to make sure we hear them correctly. That is why we make a practice of sharing what we hear.

The spiritual aspect of religion (which includes the imagination) is still the most neglected of the three. Religious controversy now and then bursts onto our headlines and screens with news of a clash between a symbolical and a literal interpretation of Christian doctrine. It is almost as though society needs the rigidity of conventional beliefs so that we can enjoy their being challenged from within the Christian community. (Spirituality is not of journalistic interest). Those who support a non-literal interpretation of doctrine are apt to be ridiculed. But doubt cannot be silenced for ever and the unconscious continues to stir in our sleep. For it is doubt, that 'precious gift', that can awaken and enrich us.

Faith is not exclusively individual. So far as Quakers are concerned, faith is the unity that encircles our diversity, a unity that can transcend doubt or disbelief and allows us to find a dynamic resolution of a disagreement. Even in mundane and practical issues this is possible if we keep our minds on our task of trying to discern what is God's will or the leading of the spirit. When, as happens occasionally, one group wants the Society of Friends to identify itself collectively with a particular policy that they have at heart, they tend to be restrained from their enthusiasm and partisan zeal and encouraged to seek unity with their fellows under the guidance of the spirit. If this tradition were to be lost, it would no longer be a religious society.

6 Perfection, Growth, Wholeness

Jung's belief that the true goal of human development is not perfection (in the religious, moral or spiritual sense) but wholeness must surely be challenged by devout Christian believers. The essence of a religious attitude is the certainty of a deity, supreme value or superhuman entity to whom we acknowledge an over-riding loyalty and with which we can to some degree identify ourselves. We experience this both outwardly and inwardly. Such a being or entity constitutes perfection. It is at once religious (outwardly), spiritual (inwardly) and moral although (as George Gorman said) we 'call it what you will'.[1] For most of us in the West, the word we use is simply God; but not for all.

Compared with this, Jung's notion of wholeness, completeness or health seems rather drab and uninspiring. Maybe it suggests some eagerness for whole-food diet, for green-peace and nature-loving environmental ideology or for physical fitness, alternative medicine, animal rights or healthy-minded psychology or muscular Christianity. All such idealisms have their followers and their value but could hardly inspire a Bach oratorio or a Mozart mass. Compared with the supremacy of religious perfection they are partisan, devoted to relative good, not to absolute, all-embracing and instrinsic good. To Jesus and his followers only God is perfect. For most Christians, the only true embodiment of the divine nature is Jesus himself, the saviour of humanity, son of God yet born of woman and conceived asexually: the only perfect human being.

For nearly two thousand years Christian doctrine has emphasized this unique duality and endorsed the ancient Jewish prophecy of a Messiah, in the conviction that Jesus was (as he proclaimed) himself that unique redeemer of humanity. He was both human and divine and also perfect. His teaching was, and still is accepted as the will of God, eternal truth. The way he lived and the values he proclaimed are the unique example of the way life should be lived, the path of perfection. To do the will of God means to follow that teaching and example as set out in the scriptures and (for most Christians) as interpreted also by the authority of spiritual guides and interpreters in the long, extensive and scholarly history of the various Churches.

For our purpose we shall consider only the very heart of this teaching about perfection and try to understand some of the implications in psychological rather than theological terms. First, however, there is a brief caution on relying too precisely on exact phraseology of the scriptures and so turning a doubt into a doctrine. We do not know the very words used by Jesus, even in translation. The sources we have, depend not only on accounts written after his death but are based on early translations from the Hebrew and Greek, from the Latin Vulgate and on versions of these in early bibles, Wycliffe's, Tindale's, Coverdale's, Matthew's and on the Great Bible of 1541, The Geneva Bible, the Bishops' Bible, the Douay Bible of 1582–1610. The loved and revered Authorized version of King James (1611) is mainly a revision of the Bishops' Bible, not a new translation. It was itself revised in 1881 and again in 1885. We now also have modern texts and new translations, Weymouth's, Moffat's, the American Revised Standard version and finally the recent New English Bible.

If we compare the use of the word 'perfect' in the King James version and the New English Bible we at once get a hint of the way religious thinking and linguistic scholarship are intertwined. The doctrine of perfection as the ultimate goal of mankind's striving and as the foundation of the Christian life can hardly be attributed with confidence to Jesus himself. In the King James version the word 'perfect' is used in this sense only twice, both times in St Matthew's gospel. One occasion is in the incident of the young man who asked what he should do to have eternal life. After saying that he had always kept the principal commandments (about murder, adultery, stealing, giving false witness and honouring one's parents and loving one's neighbour) he asked what he still lacked. Jesus

70

replied 'If thou wilt be perfect, go and sell that thou hast and give to the poor',[2] which seems to confirm the ideal of moral and religious perfection. However, when we turn to the same passage in the New English Bible we find the more matter-of-fact and less stringent 'If you wish to go the whole way, sell your possessions, and give to the poor'.[3]

The other gospel use of 'perfect' in a moral sense is in the Sermon on the Mount. It is reported both by St Matthew and by St Luke and bears interesting comparison with the New English Bible version. In the middle section of the sermon, St Matthew reports that Jesus said 'Be ye perfect, even as your Father which is in heaven is perfect'[4] (King James version). In the New English Bible his words are translated 'You must therefore be all goodness, just as your heavenly Father is all good'.[5] St Luke evidently gave a slightly different account. In the King James version the words are 'Be ye therefore merciful, as your Father also is merciful'[6] which in the New English Bible reads 'Be compassionate as your Father is compassionate'.[7]

What is suggested here (and it is no more than a suggestion) is that the insistence on striving for perfection may represent a bias of the translators of the early seventeenth century (mainly revisers rather than translators) rather than an accurate rendering of the attitude of Jesus himself. The question is worth considering not only for accuracy of translation but as a doubt whether the striving for perfection was ever an integral part of the original teaching of Jesus. In the Authorised version of the Epistles the word is used in this moral sense some fifteen times. In only five of them does the New English Bible use 'perfect' or 'perfection' as the King James scholars did. Instead we find 'full strength', 'mature', 'ripe in conviction', 'balanced character', 'fully proved'.

Maybe such change of emphasis suggests that the characteristic Puritan vision of life as a dutiful and relentless striving towards personal perfection is an unintended distortion of the original version of what Jesus taught. A grim, tight-lipped, joyless and perpetual struggle for perfection and righteousness is contrary to much of the kindly and tolerant attitude of Jesus towards human frailty and contrary to the general spirit of his teaching. Fastidious righteousness was often the butt of some of his fiercest denunciation and he certainly did not mince words in his scolding of Scribes and Pharisees.

Towards the end of the 1972 Swarthmore lecture, Richard Peters (Professor of the Philosophy of Education in London university) commented most helpfully on the Puritan tradition and the Quaker way. In one of many striking phrases, he said 'There are few whisky priests in our midst, but we have our full share of Pharisees'.[8] The numbers may have changed, of course, since then. We seem to be less strictly abstemious and rather less formally correct as time goes on. Yet the appeal of personal perfection remains among us as an ideal and moral progress as the path towards it. From a human and psychological point of view we continue to ask what we must do if, like the wealthy young man in the Gospel, we wish 'to go the whole way'. There is no lack of Christian authorities to guide, direct and instruct us if we want to listen. For Quakers there is also the inner light to guide us.

Some religions and some sects still insist on a rigid code of ritual practice to ensure progress. To the psychotherapist, such observances are somewhat suspect, whether religious or secular. Today it is widely accepted that the need for rigid formality of behaviour and repetitive ritual may be partly a matter of temperament (the so-called obsessional personality) and may also screen unconscious guilt and a fear of reprisal. It is this latter factor that concerns us here. Many of us cherish some little quirks of superstition, harmless rituals to ward off trouble, formalities that give us a sense of belonging and security, practices that help us to feel good as we repeat them—and a little uneasy if we forget or are prevented. Traditionally we have regarded ritual and formality as unnecessary and irrelevant but we still keep up our own minor observances. We can sometimes make a formality of avoiding formalism or make a ritual of rejecting ritual. Dress, habits of speech, seating arrangements, forms of address, what we eat and drink or refuse to eat and drink, games we will play and games we will not play—what are these but symbols of unity in goodness? They tend to be reassuring but, as with any fetish, they may displace the reality of our task and provide a welcome diversion of attention from the true goal. If they give us a feeling of virtue or security without requiring any effort of thought or decision they become just little indulgencies and distractions. They have their uses, but are not a true part of the Quaker way or the religious life and we may come to give them an importance they do not merit.

The solemnity with which rituals may be performed and repeated suggests that they can be used as a defence against responsibility. Hence the rigour with which they are observed and the fear that if omitted something truly awful will result. The very pursuit of moral and spiritual perfection can become a ploy to keep the attention from straying into ways that are unconsciously felt to be wicked or dangerous, temptations to be evaded rather than faced. Religious observances may be used in this way, but do not have to be.

Many of the early Puritans were rebels against formality, ritual and religious authority. They trod a somewhat solitary path to personal salvation on their own responsibility, not at secondhand or because they were constrained by the religious hierarchy of the time. As Richard Peters said of them, each was 'a spiritual aristocrat who sacrificed fraternity to liberty. In his search for perfection he shut off his spirit from the love of God and of his neighbour'.[9] He described the Puritan quest for salvation as a 'denial of the possibility of love'.[10] The striving for personal salvation and moral perfection are incompatible with humour, joy, relaxation and a glad response to beauty and the imagination, to works of art and to the creative quality of play. ('Dost thou think, because thou art virtuous, there shall be no more cakes and ale?').[11] The dour Puritan does not usually stay content to tread the path without trying to make others follow. But I do not think this is what Richard Peters understood by fraternity in that quotation from his lecture. The liberty of conscience sought so bravely by the Puritans and the freedom to practise their religion as they thought best did not of themselves isolate them from other worshippers. Isolation was due to their zeal for individual salvation and their own understanding of what constitutes perfection. Today we can hardly doubt that this zeal, courageous as it certainly was, sprang from unconscious fear of the power of evil that lurked in the shadow.

In spite of these limitations, the Puritan spirit and the striving for perfection were not wholly inhibiting. Perfection is an ideal that may inspire us to fulfil our own potential, either in practical ability or in the development of personality—what Jung termed individuation. There are many kinds of perfection and to fasten one's ambition to one that is entirely unrealizable is disheartening and may lead us to substitute outward tokens of rectitude as a cover for a sense of failure. Then we are apt to become touchy and vulnerable to not being accepted. We may be over-ambitious for merit and try to live beyond our capacity for virtue. That can lead to whisky, but Pharisaism is more likely.

The fraternity that Richard Peters referred to is much treasured by Quakers, not only as natural friendliness, good as that is. It also provides an essential safeguard against overweening confidence in our own insight and a failure to realize that the flash of understanding that may come to us is possibly misguided or based on misapprehension and needs to be tested by sharing. 'Our "inner light" (he said) is our individual perspective; but, like all light, it is not private to ourselves'.[12] We may see it indistinctly and mistake what it is we see. This is why we share our insight in worship or in a business meeting. Some people, coming to Meeting for Worship for the first time, feel rather lost without the assertions they have been accustomed to hearing in some more authoritarian denomination. Quaker ministry may strike them as vague and indecisive, lacking the self-assurance of those who assert that this or that 'is what God wants us to do'. But patient seeking for truth is really a strength, enabling us to share and develop such insight as comes to us. And this should help us to avoid arrogant certainty in matters that are not clear or simple.

Richard Peters's lecture, admirably lucid and constructive as it is, does not perhaps make quite enough allowance
for the influence of unconscious factors in the interplay of
personalities or within the individual. That was not the
aim of his lecture and he spoke as a philosopher and
educationist, not as a psychotherapist. Nevetheless, in one
passage he refers to 'the awesome spectacle of human
beings trying to make some sort of sense of the world and
trying to sustain and cultivate a crust of civilization over a
volcanic core of atavistic emotions',[13] a figure of speech that
no analyst would object to and which might indeed have
been said by Freud himself.

In Jung's view the 'volcanic core' is twofold, comprising
both the repressed shadow side of the individual psyche
and also the collective unconscious common to all of us.
The contribution that the pioneers of analysis made to this
situation (which grows ever more threatening) is not an
attempt to strengthen the 'crust' over the core but to find
how the volcanic emotional energy can be put to constructive use. In essence the way is simple, though certainly not
easy.

We can see how unrealistic and futile it would be to
advocate a perpetual struggle for moral perfection as a
means of keeping the lid on the crater, provided we can
accept the reality of the unconscious and realize that
repressed urges and feelings are very much alive in the
shadows and are liable to erupt in defiance of morality
through our feelings and take us by surprise. Moreover, if
Jung was right in maintaining that all truly constructive
developments originate in phantasy and spring into life
from the tension of opposites, it is clear that the turmoil
within is a lively source of creativity, not to be shunned as
wholly bad.

Such a view provides a revolutionary alternative to the
bitter antagonism of opposites felt to be mortal adversaries: conscious and unconscious, good and evil, creation
and destruction, black and white, male and female. This
positive attitude only frightens us if we still believe that
whatever lies in the shadow must be evil and threatening.
If we can learn to regard the unconscious as potentially

either good or bad we can learn what it has to say to us. Then the resulting spark of opposites can be the source of originality and fresh insight. But we must take it as it comes, remembering that it happens to us and that our conscious moral judgment comes into its own only when the energy is released. To try to impose a moral censorship on what comes into consciousness, to regard feelings as good or bad in themselves, is to seek to deny ourselves the gift of originality and psychic energy. To do this in the name of moral perfection is the tragedy of Puritanism.

This contrast to conventional religious and moral teaching is so important an aspect of Jung's contribution to the Quaker way that I feel constrained to offer two illustrations of how it can work in practice.

The source of the first example I have not been able to trace. It was quoted in a book review and I do not give it verbatim. A young girl had been referred to a child guidance clinic and was seen weekly by the psychiatrist. After a while her inner feelings of aggression began to surface and one day, in a sudden outburst of fury she shouted at the doctor 'I hate you! and I wish you were dead!'[14] (At this point let us have an interval to think how to reply to her. If we think in two-dimensional and moral terms we might voice our disapproval of such an outburst towards someone who was patiently trying to help her, and tell her she should learn to master such feelings that are the cause of so much havoc in the world, that she should be ashamed of such a feeling and still more at such ingratitude and bad manners. We might try to make her feel thoroughly ashamed and make her apologise. Or alternatively, we might feel that such an unwarranted outburst must be evidence that she is in a bad way, a potentially troublesome little demon who has probably never been properly loved and appreciated. We would then respond in compassion rather than anger or disapproval, doing what we can to be warmly accepting and affectionate towards her in the hope that our kindheartedness will somehow dissipate her bitter feelings.)

In the event the doctor did not see it in these terms or actively intervene but, attending to what she had said

76

without reacting to it, awaited what would follow. There was a short silence and then she said firmly *'But you better not be dead before next week.* I might change my mind.'[15] By remaining silent and receptive he was able to answer that of God in his young patient which the two other acts of intervention would have smothered.

The second example is general, familiar to any counsellor or psychotherapist whose task it is to try to help people in the kind of difficulty usually referred to as being incompatible. This means that the immediate source of friction between two people does not come solely from outer circumstances (which may suit them both very well) but from within the relationship, each thinking the other is to blame. 'I used to love him (or her) but now I don't' is the way it is usually expressed.

A careful and prompted exploring of the relationship often brings to light a paradox, that the things now most bitterly complained of in the partner are the very qualities that were originally the most attractive. For instance, she was attracted by his calm and coolness but now hates him for being cold and uncaring. Or (in another example) he was first delighted by her spontaneous erotic warmth and is now exasperated that she is so demanding. Or she admired his careful and responsible attitude to money and now finds him intolerably mean and fussy. Or he was charmed by her carefree generosity and is now maddened by her extravagence and irresponsibility. Or she rejoiced in his initiative and leadership, the way he would stand up for himself, and now resents his overbearing bossiness. Or he rejoiced in her quiet, placid manner but now calls her dull and boring and lifeless.

At a two-dimensional, common-sense, advice-giving level these very common situations seem baffling and hopeless. What advice can one give? Centred around the issues most complained of there lie strong, unconscious feelings that emerge disguised as resentful criticism of the partner. The issue (money or sex or leadership or anything else that arises) has some very special importance, some subjective meaning for the one who is now complaining.

The issue almost certainly was a factor in deciding what kind of person was found most attractive in personality. It is often as though we unconsciously seek those who will compensate for some inner difficulty or shortcoming of our own that we have never been able to face. They will perhaps take the burden off our shoulders.

Sometimes the attraction is curiously the reverse of the qualities we most admire consciously and we are attracted by what we fear, dislike and scorn. All these arise from our own unconscious shadow. They are aspects that will not leave us alone because we do not face them, cannot face them. So they are sought in others on whom our feelings are projected, temporarily freeing us from the inner threat of having to recognize them in ourselves. So we are elated. But the issue has not gone away. To the extent that it was within our own shadow, it still is. We are only hiding from it, not resolving it. And so our partner on this issue becomes a scapegoat just as (on the same or a quite different issue) we become for our partner. No wonder personal relationships can get into a vicious circle of mutual recrimination, as happens in most domestic quarrels.

These troubles make sense once we recognize that our strongest conscious feelings have their opposites in the personal unconscious. Indeed they may derive much of their strength from repression, that is to say keeping the lid on the volcano. This is often recognizable among people who hold fanatical views, for which they will fight in season and out of season and with whom friends say 'There is no discusssing that topic'. The result of patient and sensitive exploring of such issues, without any moral blame or praise, is not (as one might expect) that the individual veers over to the opposite extreme. It is that the issue loses its irrational emotional charge and can be tackled reasonably and firmly. It is no longer a red rag, nor has one red rag been exchanged for another. People then tell a counsellor, 'Somehow it doesn't bother me any more—it's no longer such an issue between us.'

Emotionally-charged conflicts may arise in any close relationship, disputes, arguments, conflicts in which strong feelings are aroused and cool reason flies away. We find our own ways of dealing with them most of the time and they give life and zest and interest to a relationship. But occasionally one of these will blow-up into a vicious circle because in some obscure and opposite way it is a problem for each participant and each tries to off-load it onto the other. Then the help of a trained third-party, concerned but unpartisan, can help to restore a living and working harmony, possibly through learning to quarrel constructively.

But it is always difficult and painful for a sincere Christian to quarrel without guilt, to tolerate the internal pressure of aggressive feelings, to recognize that the moral pressure of two-dimensional rectitude must be laid aside if reality is to be faced. The Christian virtues of tolerance, long-suffering, acceptance and submissive meekness cannot be magically or even prayerfully induced to fit an ideal of perfection until the inner issues have been brought into the light and been faced realistically. And then what a relief a good strong quarrel can provide! And how wonderfully fruitful it is to make it up. Human relationships cannot be separated from emotion, much of it conscious and much unconscious, and cannot be adjusted and developed by thought alone or at the dictate of duty or moral idealism.

'In favour of an ideal image, (wrote Jung) into which one would prefer to mould oneself, too much that is generally human has to be sacrificed'.[16]

That is to say, to cultivate an ideal of perfection necessarily means rejecting the shadow. The effect on others can be devastating, not only from a psychological point of view but from a Christian point of view also. 'To have to live with a saint can cause an inferiority complex or even a wild outbreak of immorality in individuals who are morally less gifted'.[17] That is the sad result of too much virtuousness, too much uprightness, that have been cultivated or imposed artificially in the pursuit of moral perfection and without due cognizance of all the opposite qualities that have been repressed into the personal unconscious and may erupt so unexpectedly.

Clergy, elders (and all Quakers), counsellors, social

workers, psychotherapists, doctors, teachers, psychiatrists and all good Christians are specially at risk to the baleful influence their altruism may have on their own family. Saints can make sinners of their children or spouses. It is perhaps comforting that people love us more for our weaknesses than for our virtues or strength. Progress along the path of perfection always carries a risk of smugness, self-satisfaction, arrogance masquerading as humility, or a desperate sense of personal failure when we cannot live up to our ideal.

No wonder Jung suggested wholeness as a goal rather than perfection. This is valid at all stages of life, a child should be a child, an adult should be an adult, an old person should be an old person and not an imitation young one. Each of us should seek the personal wholeness that is our own unique identity of mind, body, psyche and soul. In this sense growth is as continuous as the growth of a tree, and seasonal too. It is a natural process, not a moral achievement. 'Without the experience of opposites (wrote Jung) there is no experience of wholeness'.[18] That is the challenge to the Puritanical ideal of perfection.

7 Balance and Stability

In Chapter 2 we briefly considered ways in which the unconscious can influence us. We must now look again at the interplay of the two aspects of our mind, conscious and the unconscious shadow, because this is fundamental to Jung's teaching and has far-reaching implications for the Quaker way.

Our human consciousness is, of course, part of our biological inheritance and in some respects it is similar to the consciousness of higher animals. They are able, in some obscure way, to work out a problem and find a solution. For instance, I recall three little examples such as anyone may have observed. The first was a dog who rushed growling upstairs to get a better view of a trespassing cat outside, which he could see more clearly from a bedroom chair under a window. How did he think that out?

The second example was also of a dog. He had buried a bone in a flower-bed but on this occasion he could not settle down afterwards. Something was on his mind. Finally, he went out again, dug up the bone and re-buried it in a safer place. Might not we have done the same?

A third example was at the London Zoo. A visitor threw a banana onto the wire top of a chimpanzee's cage. He could see it and could climb up to it but could not get it through the wire mesh. He climbed down and fetched from his bedding a straw some nine inches long. With this he poked the banana violently bit by bit towards the front of his cage and finally over the edge so it fell to the ground. Here he could get his hand through the bars, reach the banana and enjoy it.

Obviously these intelligent creatures did not think in words or theories. They were able to use their memory and apply what they remembered to a new problem. Maybe much of our intelligence works in the same way, though we certainly do think in words as well as images. Perhaps they somehow think mainly in smells, sights and sounds and can recall sense experiences as we often do in dreams. Most of our human problems involve other factors than the kind of intelligence used by animals. We not only think but know that we think. We are not only conscious, as they are, but we are conscious of self. We know that we know. We make judgments not only of external events and other people but of ourselves. We have a 'knowledge of good and evil',[1] as the Authorised Version puts it.

We often make moral judgments by thinking of alternatives, such as good or evil, right or wrong, beautiful or ugly, true or false, us or them. As with perfection, each alternative is an extreme. We make assessments between them in order to choose or act, to decide whom to support or resist, what to prefer, when to intervene. These values give us boundaries and provide scales for our judgment.

Our very problems are often of two opposite kinds, intellectual and emotional, thinking and feeling, practical and theoretical, inner and outer. Our choices and decisions are usually compromises made in the 'grey area' between extremes of judgment, unless we are fanatics for whom only an extreme is acceptable. Sometimes experience presents us with a dilemma, that is to say two alternatives each of which we feel is impossible or unacceptable. 'I can't live with my husband but can't leave him because of the children'. We feel there are only two alternatives and we can't do either. Personal problems have a way of ending up as dilemmas and then we are put under severe emotional pressure. If someone advises adopting one alternative, they provoke us into being advocates for the other. If they ask then why not adopt that one, we reverse our previous view.

This process is normal and common when we are faced with an issue that is not only evenly balanced in all our scales of relevant judgment but is also of great significance for us in emotional terms. Those who try to help with advice become frustrated and sometimes, in exasperation, tell us 'Well, you must make up your own mind. I can't do that for you'. We can but reply 'But that is just what I can't do'. There cannot be many people who have never suffered this see-saw, ding-dong experience. With issues that are not of great importance to us emotionally, there is far less difficulty. We are usually able to consider more than just two opposing alternatives and our anxiety and frustration are much less stimulated. We do not expect to make a perfect decision or find an ideal solution.

In Anthony Storr's Introduction to his selection from Jung's collected works, he commented 'Human beings, because of the nature of thought and language, are bound to categorize things as opposites'.[2] The way we do this is peculiar to each of us and subjective, particularly in connection with problems of feeling rather than of thinking. We soon discover how differently others see our difficulty when we tell them about it. We usually feel they understand it only if they happen to see it in much the same way that we do. We do not believe our feelings can be mistaken and, in a sense, we are right in this, because they are our own, they are facts and are real, whether someone else thinks they are reasonable or unreasonable.

In the early years of his career, Jung was impressed with how differently individuals react to the same events. Counsellors and psychotherapists, who are used to hearing people express their feelings, have the same experience. You have to know someone intimately before you can even guess how any unforeseen experience will affect them.

As the early group of analysts, under Freud's leadership, explored ever more fully and sensitively people's unconscious reactions, these discrepancies and idiosyncrasies became ever more vivid. Jung was impressed by evidence that the same applied to the analysts themselves. He, Freud, Adler, Stekel, Reich, Brill, Ernest Jones and others interpreted similar phenomena in their own particular ways. Evidently, psychoanalysis could not be regarded as a wholly objective science and different theories were to be regarded as different approaches to the inner mysteries of personality. This view was not wholly acceptable to Freud himself and it was finally a factor in the break-up of the original tightly-knit group.

Adler made a basic distinction between a neurotic and a

delinquent attitude to life (approximating to the popular alternative reactions of Fight or Flight) that was characteristic of those who could not adjust to circumstances and were deficient in fellow-feeling. Freud (as mentioned earlier) made a primary distinction of attitude according to an emotional and attitudinal fixation at one of the normal stages of psychosexual development.

Independently of the analysts, other investigators have formulated other schemes (Kretschmer and Sheldon for example), sometimes based on physiological or temperamental factors. As psychological and neurological tests have become more sophisticated (especially with the development of projection tests), so type differences have become more precisely differentiated. Here, of course, we are concerned with Jung's views.

Jung introduced the terms introversion and extraversion (so spelt from the Latin 'extra' meaning outside). These words have become popularised but, as with other psychological terms, in not quite the correct sense. Today 'extravert' is often taken to mean a warm and friendly, outgoing attitude, down-to-earth, practical, a good mixer, amusing, jolly. And 'introvert' is usually taken, in ordinary conversation, to mean withdrawn, neurotic, highbrow, deep and unfriendly—a suspicious combination. Extraverts are generally felt to be desirable socially, introverts to be somewhat arrogant, aloof and unfriendly. It is important for us to understand the sense in which Jung used both these terms.

They were explained and contrasted by him in some of his earlier work (around 1920–30) and remained a permanent feature of his scheme. He did not use either term as necessarily praiseworthy or derogatory. To him they represented two opposite ways in which individuals regard the world and interpret their experience of it. The words also distinguish between two contrasting scales of value by which personal judgments are made and different meanings given. The extravert's view of life is objective in the sense of being concerned with external objects, tending to regard people as things and therefore in an essentially practical way.

'Self-communings (said Jung of the extravert) give him the creeps'.[3] For the introvert, 'self-communings are a pleasure':[4] he is thoughtful, solitary, used to abstract thinking, not a man of action. Each attitude has its positive and negative aspects, its advantages and disadvantages for the individual himself and for others. Each fits well into some circumstances and badly into others. Each group have their own type of successes and failures and their admirers and detractors. Each have their strengths and their weaknesses. (The popular view that the one is much better than the other is a distortion, characteristic of the general social orientation of the time).

Aldous Huxley considered this polarity of view (outwards or inwards) as too limited.[5] He preferred a classification into three main divisions (following Sheldon) and gave as conveniently typical instances Hamlet, Hotspur and Falstaff respectively. (He could as effectively have given examples of three women characters). The first of these is a typical introvert, the two others being different kinds of extravert, Hotspur pugnacious (based on his muscular system), Falstaff being self-indulgent and voluptuous (based on his gut).

Any responsible system of human typology has its limitations and its fascination and dangers. It is hard to refrain from speculating as to which label best fits our acquaintances and ourselves, so that we indulge in pigeon-holing instead of responding. Nevertheless (as with psychological testing in general) type-fixing has practical uses in skilled hands. But insight, not categorizing, is more helpful in understanding anybody. For us here the importance of Jung's two types is not for type-fixing but as an example of the interplay of opposites in human nature.

Any such division is immediately complicated by that other fundamental duality, conscious and unconscious (accepted by all psychotherapists, not only followers of Jung). Nothing can be conscious and unconscious at the same time. They are as distinct as heads and tails. But it would be facile to suppose anyone is wholly extraverted or introverted. Most of us tend towards one rather than the other in most of our reactions to people, objects and events and also in our tastes and values, our interests and ambitions. But sometimes we may unexpectedly show features of the opposite.

Jung made the important discovery that the more obviously and consciously extraverted we are, the more strongly introverted we shall be in the unconscious, personal shadow. For many people this is rather much to swallow, especially if applied to themselves. The suggestion may seem absurd and, worse still, insulting. We mostly pride ourselves on being whichever we consciously are, because we only know what is conscious. The strongly oriented introvert is not likely to take kindly to the suggestion that there is within him (or her) a jolly, show-off, practical, active, good-mixer, trying to get out. But his dreams may confirm it and so may his problems and maybe symptoms, too. So may his reading and the programmes he most enjoys watching, the historical characters that most interest him, the plays he likes best.

The evidence for this looking-glass state of affairs comes not only from dreams and phantasies and leisure interests but also from the sometimes quite desperate anxiety with which we assert its absurdity and dismiss it as ludicrous nonsense. 'What me, having an introverted side? You must be crazy'. (Or the reverse, of course, except that the introverted person would be more likely to express it differently, such as 'I don't think that is a view that I can accept').

What has been said earlier in this chapter about the severe pressure we may suffer from opposite features in a dilemma or an emotional conflict, (parts of which are likely to be unconscious) is not to be under-estimated in the havoc pressure can make in daily life till the conflict is resolved or the decision taken. (Laurence Sterne vividly described 'what a plaguing thing it is to have a man's mind torn asunder by two projects of equal strength, both obstinately pulling in a contrary direction at the same time,'[6] and most of us have known it). Considering how often our complicated lives demand our making a judgment, it is a wonder how often and regularly we are able to resolve these crises and how rarely we do get stuck in some insoluble vicious-circle and have to get expert help. We owe to Jung an understanding of how it is that we cope so effectively.

In the last chapter we touched on Jung's insistence on growing towards psychic wholeness rather than wilfully trying to make progress towards perfection. This is no hair-splitting difference. Individuation (as he termed natural psychic growth) is a natural process and should not be equated with therapy nor with conscious moral effort. It involves the whole psychic entity, not just intelligence or emotional maturing. It therefore includes the opposites that concern us here, the introverted and the extraverted sides of each personality.

The natural process of individuation, then, has its own spontaneous way of dealing with the clash of opposites that are within the psyche and those that originate in outer experience but cause inward anxiety or frustration. After all, we do not suffer a neurosis every time we are confronted by two opposite projects of equal strength or by strong and mixed feelings about someone or something, or by the stream of choices, distinctions, judgments and decisions that we are constantly making, mostly without much thought. Nor are we made ill every time violent feelings arise in us that we cannot allow ourselves to express or do not approve of or that scare or shame us. Somehow things get settled or do settle. We sober down or cheer up or get inspired or we think things over, take advice and find an answer, sometimes very successfuly, sometimes indifferently, and sometimes mistakenly or even disastrously. Even at the worst, the thing is settled— and a different set of problems follows; and even that is better than being stuck for ever with the same one, because with vicious circles the inner tension increases fast and it is then that we may develop a neurosis, (which Jung regarded as an attempt to solve an insoluble problem).

A simple and reasonably accurate way to regard this achievement of psychic growth is to think in terms of balance. It is not a question of weighing two parts of a dilemma in some moral, intellectual, religious or common-sense balance and putting in a bit more of whatever is missing from one scale—a bit more determination or clear-headedness, patience or love.

If I may be allowed a rather fanciful illustration, I instance a pair of scales in one of which is a full-grown mouse and in the other a young one. The scale goes down one side and up at the other. But wait a few weeks and the balance will get more or less equalised. How? Why? What has happened? We can give what answer we choose, it is life or growth or nature or natural development or what-ever it is that makes things develop. The problem was a difference of weight, and also a difference of time, of age. One had reached maturity, which includes weight, and the other had not; have patience, give it a chance and it will also reach maturity, and attain adult mousehood. That is to rely on Tao, the Way. It cannot solve all problems in the way we want them solved. But it can allow things to happen that we cannot make happen (though sometimes we can help). Growth and healing are examples—physical and psychological and spiritual. 'There is no energy unless there is a tension of opposites'[7] wrote Jung (and Adler might have said it, too). 'Life is born (he also wrote) only of the spark of opposites'.[8]

Jung used two terms in this connection which, in the English translation, may be confusing. One is compen-sation and the other is opposition. As both are important concepts for our purpose here, it is necessary to clarify them. The first one, compensation, in psychological use is different from the legal term, in which someone seeks compensation for an injury or tort. It is used in the rather different sense of seeking balance rather than justice, as when we speak of compensating for a feeling of weakness by some show of strength, or for a sense of sin by a show of virtue or for feeling unloved by collecting rare objects. This is to try to redress a psychic balance, by supplying the compensating or opposite factor.

As for the word opposition, it brings associations of hostility, aggression, controversy, bickering in parliament, arguing in debate, burning effigies, sending in the troops, shouting back or shouting down. In Jung's use it simply means counterpoise, something that restores and equalises balance, and so achieves stability. Thus Jung wrote 'A psychological theory, if it is to be more than a technical makeshift, must base itself on the principle of opposition'.[9] In particular and most importantly, it must be based on the opposition of conscious and unconscious factors. He continued: '... There is no balance, no system of self-regulation, without opposition. The psyche is just such a self-regulating system'.[10] The attitude of the conscious is compensated (without our active participation) by the attitude of the unconscious so that the psyche is kept in balance. Sometimes this is achieved by what are technically known as defence-mechanisms, by which we rigorously assert the opposite of what the unconscious seeks to express and so bring about an unstable equilibrium with the opposition kept in the shadow. The human psyche is self-regulating in its ability to restore the balance of opposites when it is disturbed. But it is the tension of opposites, whether conscious or not, that (according to Jung) is the source of psychic energy which we can then put to use in accordance with our own judgment. 'We can take the theory of compensation (wrote Jung) as a basic law of psychic behaviour'.[11] The conscious is compensated by the unconscious.

A simple illustration will show this law in action. If a wife tells a counsellor 'I love my husband' there is no occasion to doubt her word, no matter what their difficulties are. But if she keeps on saying it a counsellor begins to wonder why. It is unlikely that she is consciously lying because one lie would be enough. She is probably trying to convince the counsellor, because she fears the evidence of many quarrels might make her statement hard to believe. Or something else may be happening: she may be trying to convince herself. Why? Because her unconscious is trying to assert the fact that she can hate her husband as well as love him.

Such mixed and opposite feelings are common in any close relationship. And common, too, especially among devout Christians is intense guilt about hostile feelings towards those it is one's religious duty to love. Hence the imbalance and the pressure from the unconscious to bring about a better balance. But that is to make an admission that would be guilt-laden so it must be kept at bay by assurances to the contrary. This state of affairs may be so tense as to be emotionally explosive. It requires delicate, sympathetic and morally-neutral handling by the counsellor or therapist. The self-regulating activity of the psyche needs time and a sympathetic atmosphere for its healing task. To take sides with her feelings of love or of hate for her husband would hinder the process. To try to support her unrealistic ambitions as a perfect wife who is never furious with her husband would inhibit progress towards a new and more realistic balance. We are back once more at the sorry propensity of religious people to attach moral blame to certain emotions. This applies not only in a consulting-room but in the daily social and family contacts of ordinary life.

As we develop our own scale of values to help us make the necessary judgments required by daily life, we tend to develop habitual attitudes of approval and disapproval between a large number of opposite qualities. Jung regarded the self as a hypothetical mid-point between conscious and unconscious whose function is to ensure 'that conscious and unconscious demands are taken into account as far as possible'.[12]

This enables us to establish our own characteristic way of dealing with the conflicts, dilemmas and decisions of normal life and to develop what Adler called our style-of-life, that is, a kind of theme or motif or character that we express in our decisions and relationships, at once the result of compensations and opposition and the guide-lines that we have slowly formed for ourselves.

In this way we evolve a useful ethical and emotional and idealistic system of our own (not taken secondhand) to guide us through the exceedingly complex process of daily life and constant demands on us to make evaluations. If it can be kept subject to revision, such an internal compass can serve us well and save a great deal of anxiety. But it has a disadvantage also. Our emotional and moral attitudes become persistent to the extent that they serve us well. This makes it difficult for us to adapt our attitude to new conditions in which, perhaps, it is not adequately relevant. 'A man's attitude to reality (wrote Jung in an early paper) is something extraordinarily persistent'.[13] This may make difficulties for him. He may find it hard or impossible to adapt to environmental demands and unexpected changes. Such a hold-up obstructs one's growth towards psychic wholeness and maturity.

This issue of adaptation within a flexible structure of values and abilities serves to emphasize the moving, changing, developing nature of psychic life. And, in turn, contrasts with the ideal of steady moral progress towards religious perfection. It means that the balance we have been referring to is not a final and rigid condition, once achieved and then safeguarded. Rather it is a constantly renewed process, no sooner reached than adapted and modified in fresh circumstances, yielding a changing and growing way of life and of judgment, gradually developing and maturing but never completed, never perfected.

This ever-moving process of psychic growth, attaining different kinds and degrees of wholeness at each stage of life and in changing circumstances, is more mobile and less rigid than most conventional moral and religious teaching about virtues and vices, temptation and grace, progress, righteousness and final perfection and a static eternity. It was, I think, eloquently summed-up in a mere five words of the poet laureate (and doctor) Robert Bridges: 'Our stability is but balance'.[14]

By way of analogy I offer a little picture from a school gymnasium or a leisure-centre. A child walks along an upturned horizontal gymnastic beam, a foot or two from the ground. Her arms are stretched out at either side. She looks steadily ahead, feeling her way toe-first and step by step along the beam, keeping her balance by moving her arms, restoring her stability whenever it is threatened, not so as to stay still in one place, but so as to get to the other end. Her stability is balance and her balance must be maintained if she is to reach the end.

These insights of Jung's have a helpful and constructive bearing on Quaker Meeting for Worship which can provide a unique religious setting for their application. The normal tolerant and relaxed and attentive atmosphere, the thoughtful and unhurried reflection, the fact that most people present know one another well, the courteous tradition of not interrupting and of allowing time to consider every point that is expressed—all this can be helpful in recognizing and accepting as valid opposite ideals, values and judgments. We are helped by our corporate awareness of searching together for what is right and true or (as some would prefer to express it) trying to apprehend God's will. We are not trying to win an argument or plug a partisan point of view.

All this gives those present a chance to participate silently in a balance of views and convictions expressed in ministry and to make a contribution if the call comes. At its best Meeting for Worship provides a potent atmosphere of security for achieving our own balances and stability. Then we go away refreshed, invigorated and often challenged by the experience. Every good meeting has within it some spontaneous tension arising from the awareness of opposites. It is a tension of growth and insight, not of antagonism, competition or rivalry.

Not all Sunday meetings are equally helpful, of course. The essential tension between opposite beliefs, ideals and views is sometimes unacceptable to some of those present. If people become worried that antagonism is brewing, someone will impulsively seek to soothe it. Sometimes such intervention is timely, sometimes unnecessary and inhibiting. But these are not objective assessments.

Some members may welcome the rising tension as a prelude to some spark of fresh insight or new growth of understanding; others may be disturbed by their own emotional resonance when the issue touches them too closely for comfort. It can be disturbing if someone speaks to our condition. Most Meetings are self-regulating and, in a psychological sense provide their own compensating ministry. Someone allays tension that is getting too strong, not from fear but as a natural and healing response. There is a delicate balance between tension and relaxation to which an alert meeting is sensitive. If the tension is too slack and cosy, or has been lulled out of existence by routine ministry, no one is helped to find new insight. If it is too strong or adventurous, people become anxious or potentially hostile.

Some meetings find it helpful to hold occasional separate discussions (on a weekday evening) to talk over together the purpose of ministry and the way their own meeting is working. Such discusion can be much helped by considering relevant passages in the Book of Discipline (in Chapters 7 and 24), for instance 'Vocal ministry . . . is not the utterance of careless, surface thoughts that flit through the mind, not even the sharing on a merely intellectual level of riches won from reading and reflection: it is the offering of experience won in thought and in life which . . . has led to a deeper vision of God and of his ways of dealing with men'[15]—that is, with people of all ages and both sexes. The same passage goes on to speak of 'the ministry of inspiration'.[16] The paragraphs on ministry in *Church Government* end with a summary: 'The purpose of all ministry is to lead the meeting into a closer communion with God, and into a fresh vision of the purposes he would have us pursue as we seek his kingdom'.[17] Quaker worship is not an easy concept to define but it is the essential factor that distinguishes our Sunday meetings from a group exercise in individuation or therapy. The personal wholeness towards which psychological growth is directed is spiritual and also psychological. Jung's teaching about opposites and about compensation can be most helpfully integrated into the necessary tension and balance in the religious life of our meeting, provided we accept the challenge involved in it.

Most meetings seem to be fortunate in having members with a special gift for a closing ministry. They bring together the opposites that have arisen and can wonderfully harmonise them into a new growth of understanding. They seem to have the ability themselves to accept opposites as complementary. This is not a matter of pouring oil onto troubled waters or providing a sentimental anodyne.

It is a wide offering based on the acceptance and not the rejection of complementarity so that growth may continue from one meeting to another. Professional oil-pourers, on the contrary, obstruct the lively tension and psychic growth of a meeting.

8 Images of God and of Jesus

In this chapter we shall compare Jung's understanding of these two images with the way Quakers generally see them. By 'images' I mean of course what these names bring to the mind's eye—the way we think about them rather than define them.

This is a delicate task. For Christian true believers, there is a supreme meaning and an intensity of reverence attached to both of them. In religious parlance, 'word' and 'name' themselves have a holy and numinous significance. 'In the beginning was the Word',[1] 'the Word was made flesh and dwelt among us',[2] 'the milk of the word',[3] 'the word of life'.[4] Prayers are given weight by asking 'in the name of' Jesus, sermons often begin 'In the name of' the Holy Trinity, baptism is performed 'in the Name of the Father, and of the Son, and of the Holy Ghost' in the Book of Common Prayer of the Church of England. To ask what we mean by such holy names may seem like desecration. It is, however, necessary if we are able to understand the implications of Jung's views.

Traditionally, each of these two images has been defined by ecclesiastical authorities, not by psychologists. As is well known, Freud had a somewhat dismissive, almost contemptuous opinion of religion, seeing it as neurotic wish-fulfilment to compensate for anxiety. He regarded the theories and interpretations of theologians as rationalization. The tradition of theological interpretation has nevertheless continued. Even today there are ardent controversies among Christian authorities, much popularized if they are controversial and radical. One of the most impressive scholarly landmarks of recent years has been the pair of major works of Hans Küng (professor of Dogmatic and Ecumenical Studies at the German university of Tübingen). It took him some three hundred thousand words to answer (in the affirmative) the age-old question that has exercised philosophers and theologians for centuries: *Does God Exist?* This remarkable achievement followed his equally outstanding study *On Being a Christian,* first published in 1974, and now available in a fine English translation. Both books are of impressive scholarship and admirable clarity. Both are enjoyably readable in spite of their great length. There are many other recent and widely read religious books and lectures, notably by Gerald Priestland and Don Cupitt. Such work and such publicity have kept theological concerns alive and topical. There has been activity, too, among the Society of Friends, although they are practical rather than theological in their approach to religion. The Swarthmore lecture of 1980 (by Janet Scott)[5] had the sub-title *Towards a Quaker Theology.* Many Quakers advocate a formal exposition of Quakerism, though the interest tends to be historical. (It may be of interest to note that Hans Küng listed English Quakers among possible forms of charismatic movement).[6]

By contrast with all this flood of words, Jung's lack of interest in theology and his intense interest in religion when derived from experience is most striking. It was memorably illustrated in his famous interview with John Freeman, broadcast in October 1959 in the BBC series *Face to Face.*[7] Asked whether he now believed in God, Jung tersely answered that he did not need to believe, he *knew.* He made the same distinction, on the same subject, four years earlier in another interview.[8] He often voiced a distinction between knowing by experience and believing on faith or authority.

It normally seems to be taken for granted that religion is a matter of what you believe and that only mystics, cranks and holy men have religious experience. Jung saw this matter the opposite way. For him, God is a reality, theology is theorizing about him. His reply to John Freeman should not, I think, be taken as a bold assertion of faith but as a slightly brusque reply to a question scarcely worth answering since the answer is so obvious. In general conversation 'Do you believe?' often seems to imply that you can't really.

People sometimes ask 'Did Jung believe in God?'. What matters most to us here is to understand what he meant by God and what we mean by God, because these may be very different. To the therapist something is true if it exists, if it is real. In everyday life we appeal to objective evidence. If someone is convinced the sun is shining and we are convinced it is not, we settle the matter by getting witnesses or some other evidence, like whether there are shadows. But the psychotherapist is dealing with subjective views, opinions and certainties, not simply with ascertainable facts. Meanings, ideals, aims, delusions are all real. They are true for that person at that time and a therapist had better not dispute them out-of-hand. If he does, his patient or client will 'know' that he (the therapist) is crazy and will have no more to do with him. The psychotherapist is necessarily interested in a different kind of truth from the practical person who accepts as true only what is a literal and provable fact. The importance of this distinction is not who is right but whether we accept the psyche and its manifestations as real, whether we accept that part of the human mind and personality which is not material, measurable, factual. That is to say, whether we accept the reality of the whole realm of the spiritual, the ideal, the imaginative.

Jung was constantly aware of the difference between these two points of view. For instance, he wrote 'What most people overlook or seem unable to understand is the fact that I regard the psyche as *real*. They believe only in physical facts'.[9] To disregard the psyche as having no real existence is the way of the extravert and is so common as to be normal in the extraverted age we live in, concentrating attention on external objects and tending to see people as objects. Jung continued 'They believe only in physical facts, and must consequently come to the conclusion that either the uranium itself or the laboratory equipment created the atom bomb . . .'.[10] He added 'God is an obvious psychic and non-physical fact'.[11]

If this parallel should seem at first far-fetched, we should ask ourselves who or what decided to make these bombs and who makes them and all the other horrors of warfare, mass destruction and genocide. It is the psyche of human beings that decides to do these things, actual people's minds, the individual and collective psyche of men and women, conscious and unconscious. Are they not real? In Tolstoy's great novel *Resurrection* there is a vivid and totally convincing picture of the process by which men combine their efforts and divide their responsibilities to achieve results not one of them would consider right. By bureaucratic organization no one in the whole chain of responsibility had to accept any moral blame for the outcome, however atrocious. Each simply carried out his allotted task as was his duty. In the end, results just happen of themselves, the logical and inevitable outcome of the process. Men can be trained to kill and to torture but they must first be dehumanised. Psychic events are real and can result in acts of war, torture and other horrors.

Highly intelligent and gifted people are among those who are sometimes unable to accept non-material reality. One hears them use the contemptuous phrase 'only in the mind', meaning unreal and of no account. But what evil perpetrated by one person on another was not first 'only in the mind'? God, too, is 'only in the mind' so far as our image of him goes. Jung knew differently and it is no wonder that he admitted he had to say what no one wanted to hear.

First, then, he insisted on the reality of the psyche, as an empirical fact. Secondly, God acts upon us through the psyche. But, as he wrote, 'We cannot tell whether God and the unconscious are two different entities'.[12] This last observation is disturbing to those who accept God in the conventional image of the all-loving, all-powerful creator who is timeless and was never himself created. To assert that we cannot tell whether he and the unconscious are separate entities must seem heretical. Yet it is not so far removed from the belief that God is both outside us and within, both transcendent and immanent or to believe that it is through the unconscious that God's influence can be felt directly. Perhaps we are too liable to assume that whatever emerges from the unconscious is evil and therefore cannot come from God whom we equate with the supreme good.

To Jung, the unconscious is the medium through which

God speaks. That is not to deny that evil can come in the same way. He called the unconscious 'the only available source of religious experience'.[13] He went on to say 'This is certainly not to say that what we call the unconscious is identical with God or is set up in his place'.[14] This disclaimer is important for those who suspect that Jung is really saying that God is only another name for the unconscious. This was far from being his view. He maintained that within the human psyche there is an image, an imprint of God and that, though immaterial, it is real. He did not mean this to be taken as a philosophical or theological proof of God's existence, since that is not the concern or within the scope of the psychologist. He did not mean his observations to be taken as proof of the existence of God and wrote 'They prove only the existence of an archetypal image of the Deity . . . which to my mind is the most we can assert psychologically about God'.[15] He suggested that the image of God is imprinted on the psyche as part of our personality.

Bernard Shaw once said that man creates God in his own image. That was not Jung's view. 'We do not create "God", (he wrote) we *choose* him'.[16] As a psychologist Jung was concerned with what is imprinted, not with speculating as to who did the imprinting. That is the province of the theologian. Hence Jung's persistent concern with religious experience, not with theology. He did not see religious faith as something to be worked out intellectually and consciously. 'The seat of faith (he said) . . . is not consciousness but spontaneous religious experience, which brings the individual's faith into immediate relation with God'.[17] With God, not with theological authorities. How far is this in harmony with the Quaker way?

Quakers are familiar with two forms of religious experience. One is the Inner Light or the Inner Voice, the other is the peak experience or direct awareness of the numinous in the mystical tradition. The more practical and extraverted among us have no difficulty in accepting the reality of the former which they accept as coming from God or (as some prefer to express it) from the Spirit. The more mystical-minded and introverted among us are aware of the experience of a relation of union with God or the Spirit— perhaps only fleetingly, but irresistibly and inexplicably. It is something that once experienced is never forgotten. It is authentic and indescribable. To others, this aspect of religion is suspect. In his Swarthmore lecture, for instance, Richard Peters said it was something he had 'never been able to make much of' and which seemed to him 'akin to telepathy or clairvoyance',[18] a view shared by other highly intelligent critics but incomprehensible to those who have or have had the experience. (Jung regarded thinking and feeling as opposite capacities, whichever is dominant being compensated for in the unconscious).

Jung considered the Inner Voice to be the mid-point between conscious and unconscious. But he emphasised that this view is not generally accepted. As he wrote, 'That there might be a middle point worthy of consideration [between conscious and unconscious] occurs to no one'.[19] He asserted that the medium of religious experience is not the conscious but the unconscious, in dreams, phantasies, imagination erupting as opposites of rational, conscious thinking. It is nothing strange to Quakers that these two aspects of the psyche should meet as a spark of opposites. It occurs often in Meeting for Worship. Each is valid and our most constructive ideas emerge from their interaction through the inner voice, the mid-point. In business meetings this occurs corporately, through the 'feeling of the meeting'.

For some Quakers Jung's image of God is perhaps too indistinct and impersonal to be convincing. They may perhaps feel more at home with a very different image, that of the loving, personal God, the archetypal Father of the New Testament. As a way of expressing the spiritual life this was supported by Arthur Eddington, astronomer and expounder of Albert Einstein's theory of relativity. In the Swarthmore Lecture of 1929[20] he said: 'We have to build the spiritual world out of symbols taken from our own personality, as we build the scientific world out of the symbols of the mathematician. I think therefore we are not wrong in embodying the significance of the spiritual world to ourselves in the feeling of a personal relationship'.[21] The traditional image of God as the universal Heavenly Father, as taught by Jesus, is unacceptable to many people today because of its inflexibly patriarchal character. Moreover, God is a spirit, and how can a spirit be either male or female?

In the 1980 Swarthmore lecture Janet Scott faced the problem of finding an adequate way of speaking about spiritual matters and, in particular, of God. She commented 'What we say is provisional, symbolic and metaphorical. So that when we speak of God in a personal way we do not mean that God is a person, only that personal language is the best way we have to express an inexpressible relation'.[22] She considered that the traditional way of speaking of God emphasises transcendence. 'This is the creator God of whom we use such words as majesty, power, glory, eternal, infinite, ineffable'.[23]

Another way, she said, emphasizes immanence: 'We see the whole world as in God's gracious presence and therefore holy and sacramental, drawing from us a response of reverence and care'.[24]

This image of the divine may be recognized 'in all people as they respond to life with love and trust and in the growth towards fullness of humanity'.[25] It is to be seen also 'in every act of self-sacrifice and consideration, in courage and commitment, in forgiveness and healing, in reconciliation and mercy, in the weakness of the weak and the strength of the strong'.[26] She sums up this view as 'the divine tenderness, the love and upholding, closer than heartbeats, nearer than breathing, evoking in us responsibility and gentleness and compassion'.[27] She mentions some inadequacies or insufficiencies of both these images. Regarding the second (the immanent), she says 'Thirdly, this model poses acutely the problem of evil, both of moral evil and physical suffering without having in itself any resources to solve the problem'.[28] This, in our present discussion, is a most significant limitation.

Her third model relates to the Being, or the nature, of God, which she says may be used 'not in a rational but in a mystical way'[29] and quotes Isaac Pennington's reference to 'the true peace, the true righteousness, the true holiness, the true rest of the soul, the everlasting habitation which the redeemed dwell in'.[30] She goes on to say 'However, it is more true to our Quaker experience to speak of God in terms of transitive verbs and verbs of action, as a dynamic spirit acting towards us'.[31] She takes a view similar to Jung's in 'holding the tension'[32] of these different 'models of God',[33] so that we may approach nearer to the truth. She ended her lecture with this paragraph:

'But in the end, this is the truth not of words but of response, of the living relationship of worship, love, trust and hope, of God in us and we in God, caught up out of self and out of time into the foreshadowing of what shall be and ever is. We are called to turn to that tenderest compassion, that inexpressible glory, that most profound humility, that deepest friendship, that truest vision, to the God who meets us, whom we know, in the silence, waiting'.[34]

Among these images (or models as she calls them) of God, Janet Scott rejected the customary one of the Holy Trinity on the grounds that it is based on 'a defective definition of humanity',[35] in that it is patriarchal and excludes the feminine. 'There is an urgent need (she said) for a new definition of humanity based not on patriarchal tradition nor on matriarchal fantasies but on an honest and profound study of what it means to be human'.[36] Jung's views would surely have a special relevance for any such study, most of all, perhaps, on the profoundly important issue of evil.

Jung, like Janet Scott, regarded the conventional Christian view of God as a denial of the feminine, particularly within the Protestant Churches. It is a tradition that dates back far beyond Christianity to the ancient Hebrew scriptures (as mentioned earlier). So deeply-rooted a tradition must (in psychological terms) arise from and accompany the repression of femininity into both the individual and collective unconscious. This suggestion is confirmed by the great difficulty and heart-searching involved in discussing proposals to approve the ordination of women priests. Jung would, I believe, have endorsed Janet Scott's opinion that 'The image of a masculine God is both the creation and the ideological support of a patriarchal society'.[37]

Unfortunately overt opposition to a deeply-entrenched view tends to reinforce it. It is therefore psychologically naïve to hope that this highly-charged issue can be resolved quickly, easily or by reason alone. The present stalemate polarises advocates into opposite camps and bores all those who are not partisan. Janet Scott believed also that the doctrine of the Trinity (which excludes the feminine) and the doctrine of the redemption of humanity by the death of Jesus 'inadequately represent God, the living, loving, saving spirit'.[38]

These last reflections may be taken as further evidence of the repression of femininity, though perhaps it is questionable whether 'living, loving and saving' should be regarded as exclusively feminine qualities. A sense that the loving, caring character of God is being denied by these doctrines may account for a further characteristic of contemporary Christian attitudes, namely religious sentimentality. In some parts of her lecture (already quoted) Janet Scott's language seems (at least to me) to come close to this. It occurs in Quaker ministry sometimes, where there is nothing creative, only a comforting reassurance that, for example, 'God's in his Heaven—All's right with the world!'[39] or 'All shall be well and all shall be well and all manner of thing shall be well'.[40]

The emphasis on a loving, caring, benevolent Father and Creator, characterises this type of ministry as it does some hymns and sermons in other denominations and much mystical writing. In support of it, one may point out that much (though not all) the recorded teaching of Jesus endorsed the loving, caring, supportive benevolence of the heavenly Father. If this quality is known as a fact, why does it need to be so often repeated?

It is a stark challenge to record that Jung criticized this one-sided image and saw it as evidence of the declining vitality of modern Christianity. This in turn challenges the support of those who look to religion as a source of comfort and cheer and hope and faith but not of wholeness and growth. 'Religious sentimentality (wrote Jung) instead of the numinosum of divine experience: this is the well-known characteristic of a religion that has lost the living mystery'.[41] Such a religion, he believed, has no effect and helps no one. True, but help and morality imply an acceptance of responsibility: there are times when we want comfort and reassurance, not stimulus.

Jung did not deny the good quality within the Deity—of course not. But he questioned that this is all there is. Anthony Storr records how Jung in childhood became convinced that 'God had a "dark" side which did not accord with the conventional Christian image of an ever-loving father'.[42] Jung dealt with this in some detail in his autobiographical *Memories, Dreams, Reflections* where he described the great impression made on him in his school-days by Goethe's Faust and, later, by the Book of Job. The revolutionary view that the divine nature cannot be only and wholly good, since good has no meaning without its opposite concerned Jung throughout his life and inspired much of his writing and his researches, including his remarkable short book (one of his latest works to be included in the Collected Works), *The Undiscovered Self*.

Rather than debate this issue in theological terms, let us glance at its implications. If we will have nothing to do with the suggestion that the divine nature may include goodness and its opposite, then how do we see the obvious presence of evil among and within us? Today no one can be blind to the reality, power and menace of evil. If God is wholly and absolutely good, then presumably we must see evil as either arising from some different source or within our own nature, or both. We habitually project evil onto adversaries, rivals, criminals and enemies, particularly if they are far off and not known to us personally. Our daily news bulletins and newspapers feed this propensity. As for the Devil, the Prince of Darkness, we mostly do not take him as seriously as he was formerly taken; and most Christians are not unduly affected by the doctrine of original sin, which Jung regarded as realistic and healthful.

Quakers are not prone to become involved in such issues, on two grounds. First, there is so much undeniable suffering and injustice around us and all over the world that we feel better employed trying to relieve it than asking how it has arisen or might be prevented and perhaps feeling if all were true followers of Christ it would all vanish. Secondly, these efforts (for which Quakers have a good record, as have other Christians) demand so much attention that we need not look evil in the face. In an earlier chapter I mentioned that evil has practically no place in *Christian Faith and Practice*. Religious reassurance and sometimes religious sentimentality and religious healthy-mindedness together help us to keep our minds away from evil as a ravaging and dynamic force among humanity. Do we not take a little modest pride in our cheerfulness and optimism? (Jung would not advocate the opposite but only ask if our sentiments are realistic or illusory).

In all these ways, Jung suggests, we project all goodness and perfection onto God and all evil onto scapegoats—criminals, warmongers, child abusers, addicts and the rest, leaving ourselves empty, subject to elation when our projections seem successful and to dejection when they are unsuccessful. In reality, says Jung, the individual self is the true mid-point between the opposites that are within, if only we had not forgotten how to look. To stop projecting so much of the good and the evil in our own personality (conscious and unconscious) is the first essential step in psychic growth towards wholeness.

Even the most practical among us cannot afford to ignore the perennial clash between good and evil, love and power, wholeness and divisiveness. The way we interpet these issues and the meaning they have for us affect what we do and the individual and collective attitudes we adopt. They also affect the priorities we give to the tasks that confront us. We are wise to keep clear of theological hair-splitting which too easily provides an intellectual escape from urgent moral problems of commitment. But we are not wise to neglect the fresh light that Jung's psychology can provide.

Most Quakers are ready to look afresh at the time-honoured patriarchal view. As mentioned in the first chapter, the Roman Catholic church accepted the dogma of the bodily assumption of Mary into heaven. In effect this added a fourth (and feminine) archetypal figure to the Holy Trinity, which Jung regarded as theologically epoch-making. But among the Protestant churches, the conventional view of God still remains predominantly masculine.

The second query raised by Janet Scott for her fellow Quakers is more controversial or even disquieting. This concerned the redemption of humanity by the appalling death inflicted on Jesus, the obscene cruelty of which Christians are liable to hide from themselves by religious sentimentality and the ritual veneration of the symbolic cross. The all-powerful God could have prevented this atrocious act of sacrificing his innocent son—this same God who is portrayed as all-loving and so caring that 'even the hairs of your head have all been counted'.[43]

Of course, this puzzle has troubled the minds of scholars for centuries and led to endless theological rationalization. Yet the doctrines of the *Summum Bonum* and *Privatio Boni* have long ago disposed of the Gnostic heresy that the divine nature is not wholly good. The *Privatio Boni* doctrine was dated by Jung as existing from the 4th century and from St Augustine of Hippo (died 430). It has been endorsed by Christian authorities ever since. It asserts that evil has no real existence, being merely the absence of good (privatio meaning a removal or taking away). This results in a vivid example of William James's 'healthy-minded attitude' which is blind to the existence of evil, sickness and suffering. Jung quotes an anonymous Protestant theologian as having 'the temerity to assert that "God *can* only be good" '.[44]

No doubt with the Book of Job in mind, Jung wryly commented 'Yahweh could certainly have taught him a thing or two'.[45] In his view omnipotence unavoidably places God beyond morality, as exemplified by the cat-and-mouse treatment of Job and the swaggering, bullying boasts that went with it. Jung called the Book of Job 'this great tragedy, which has never at any time lost its vitality'.[46] He commented 'The drama has been consummated for all eternity: Yahweh's dual nature has been

revealed, and somebody or something has seen and regis-
tered this fact'.[47] We are reminded that both omnipotence
and the unconscious are independent of morality.

The tragedy for human beings lies in our difficulty in
accepting a paradox (both good and evil) and seeing only
incompatible alternatives (either good or evil). We thus
deprive and relieve ourselves of responsibility for making
moral choices based on 'the knowledge of good and evil'.[48]
If God is wholly and totally good, we need decide nothing
but only obey his commandments, our worst sin being
neglect. In reality neither psychology nor religion can
absolve us from our responsibility. What happens in concentration camps, he pointed out, cannot be regarded
merely as ' "accidental lack of perfection"—it would sound
like mockery'.[49]

The problem of how we see and feel the divine nature,
both outside and within ourselves, rests on how we
respond to this problem of evil. Perhaps we must learn to
accept the mysterious and insoluble paradox. If so, all the
more reason for us first to recognize good and evil as
essential though opposite and so accept the necessity of
making our own conscious moral choices and decisions.
Jung did not claim to have resolved this question of evil
but he could rightly claim to have recognized it and
accepted it. 'In the last resort (he wrote) there is no good
that cannot produce evil and no evil that cannot produce
good,'[50] (a view hardly acceptable to the healthy-minded).

For many Christians, Jung's belief that God has a dark
side is unacceptable. It contradicts the image presented by
Jesus himself of an all-loving and all-powerful heavenly
father. Could he have been tragically mistaken, as his
dying words suggest? How can that despairing accusation
be explained away by adherents of the *Summum Bonum* and
Privatio Boni doctrines? Are the doctrines of original sin,
the fall of man, the existence and power of Satan (counterpart of the loving God, recognized and acknowledged by
Jesus)—are these adequate to explain the menace and
experience of evil that healthy-mindedness and religious
sentimentality cannot keep hidden for ever?

Such questions have teased the minds of men and women ever since it became apparent that the second coming of Jesus was not imminent. Jung's contribution to these age-old concerns is uncompromising: good and evil are inseparably linked.

All the arguments for and against dualism, all the wisdom and ingenuity of philosophers and theologians have not enabled us to bring these opposites into harmony and stop projecting our evil onto enemies, rivals and scapegoats. And since our strongest prejudices and convictions get their strength and obstinacy from unconscious projection, we would be wise to heed Janet Scott's assertion of the need for a new definition of humanity—or at least a deeper understanding of human nature and how we tick.

Many Christians respond to these insoluble conflicts by diverting faith from the image of God to an image of Jesus as portrayed in the Gospels and interpreted by Church authorities. Quite apart from the influence of any Christian upbringing and the lip-service paid throughout Western society (even by non-believers) there is no denying the charismatic influence of this magnetic figure and the appeal of his teaching, however impractical we may feel it to be in the world we know today. Jesus certainly recognized the power and inevitability of evil. Both his recorded life and his teaching present an image as compelling and irresistible as that of the Buddha. Is it not enough to follow as best we can in the steps of so exalted a master?

Unhappily, it is not. To follow and imitate that ideal figure is to externalize (by projection) that which is best from one's own personality. Instead of understanding its message we make ourselves into a mere object, a feeble replica, loyally copying an external pattern. This leaves us inwardly empty and unchanged. Hence the lifeless quality of routine religion in any denomination. To try to imitate an image that we equate with perfection is to ensure a persistent sense of failure and an unspontaneous religion lived at secondhand.

When writing of the educational function of religion, Jung said that 'religion excels all rationalistic systems in that it alone relates to the outer and inner man in equal degree'.[51] He added that we should beware of blaming Christianity for our own failure to avail ourselves of its help inwardly and outwardly. Imitation of even the highest ideal is not the path towards wholeness. 'It is not a question of imitation that leaves a man unchanged . . . but of realizing the ideal . . . in one's own individual life'.[52]

Jung described the clash between the teaching of Jesus and the power-worship of the Roman empire of his time and the deification of Caesar. The story of the temptation illustrates this clash and is of great psychological and religious significance. The temptation represented the opposition between Christianity and the worship of the emperor and his worldly power, in the mind of Jesus himself. He commented 'The religion of love was the exact psychological counterpart to the Roman devil worship of power'.[53]

Jung regarded the life of Jesus as 'the psychological prototype of the only meaningful life . . . that strives for the individual realization—absolute and unconditional—of its own particular law'.[54] However, in his view Protestantism has 'reduced the divinity of Christ to vanishing point'[55] and 'found its last refuge in the personality of Jesus'.[56]

These observations perhaps explain the contrast between Quaker Meetings for Worship. Some straightforward ministry in Christian terms is sometimes tense, vital and gripping, even when expressed falteringly; at other times it is dull, lifeless, perfunctory, sentimental and routine, even though expressed clearly and confidently. I believe the difference is that dull ministry is usually simple morality or is anecdotal and based on the human personality of Jesus as one might speak of any revered person.

By contrast, ministry that captures the inward, poetic, religious drama of tension between worldly and spiritual issues in the present and is of pressing concern to whoever is speaking—such ministry alerts the attention and rouses the concern of all who are attuned to its message. In the one instance, the image of Jesus is of an interesting and reverenced historical personality; in the other, the image is of an ideal, archetypal, symbolic figure also. In this latter sense, the birth, life, death and resurrection of Jesus are not only historical events but are deeply symbolical of spiritual issues that confront all of us today, mainly unconsciously. In the first instance, the figure of Jesus is seen as a prototype of action or behaviour or morality; in the second, it acts upon us inwardly as a symbol and a challenge.

9 Personality and Persona

Quaker worship influences how we behave towards other people, both individually and collectively.

To most other worshippers the Quaker Meeting for Worship is not worship at all. It gives no outward, visible and audible praise to the Almighty, expresses no gratitude for the blessings of life, makes no dutiful resolution to obey God's law or follow Christian ideals. It confesses no failure or need for forgiveness and help and it confirms no articles of formal belief.

In the Quaker tradition, worship combines contact with the numinous (or awareness of God's presence undistracted by externals) with concern to act on it for the general good. Our duty to God is to be sensitive to his promptings and to care for our neighbours. Like the Puritan, John Milton, most Quakers feel (I believe) that 'God doth not need Either man's work or his own gifts'.[1] As William Penn put it, 'True godliness don't turn men out of the world, but enables them to live better in it, and excites their endeavours to mend it'.[2]

A preparatory document (circulated before a Quaker conference on Industry and the Social Order) contained a far-reaching extension of this idea of practical godliness that had inspired much pioneer social welfare. 'Besides the need for right material conditions (it said) there is the at least equally vital need of right personal relationships, of all that is involved in loving one's neighbour'.[3] (It seems strange today to note that this extract is the only reference to personal relationships noted in the index to *Christian Faith and Practice*).[4] This development reflected the growing concern in Western society with relationships and the proliferation of voluntary and statutory (religious and secular) organizations to implement that concern. Social Science, Social Anthropology and Social Psychology, as well as Industrial Welfare, all combined to give state-organized expression to the new concept of 'the welfare state' and the 'caring society'.

Christianity has always, of course, emphasized the duty of loving one's neighbour. The parable of the Good Samaritan (recorded only in Luke's gospel) has always had an unequalled hold on the altruism of all normal people, whether Christian or not. Even now, when the most we can often do for a victim is to dial 999, we feel guilty if we have 'passed by on the other side',[5] however busy. For Christians (as for many others) love and compassion are supreme values but are now known to be not wholly within our control. Like all feelings, goodwill cannot be felt to order. It is not entirely subject to the conscious will so cannot reasonably be demanded as a duty. Thanks to the depth psychologists, we now know far more than previously about the influence of unconscious urges, reactions and motives and their effect on relationships. Today, the simple phrase 'all that is involved in loving one's neighbour'[6] is seen to require a formidable feat of understanding.

In the Swarthmore lecture of 1944, the Quaker neurologist W. Russell Brain took this issue a most significant stage further. In explaining the contribution that psychology can make to a deeper understanding of relationships (and hence of religion), he wrote 'The main function which psychology can perform for the individual is to enable him to know himself better, and to see more clearly the way in which his thinking and feeling are influenced by unconscious motives, and, so far as he sees this, to make allowance for it and correct it, and to recognize the limitation and partiality of his point of view even when thus corrected'[7]. This quotation has been given Quaker endorsement by being included in *Christian Faith and Practice*—so far as I know the only reference therein to the unconscious. Nevertheless it is necessary to add that to the practising analyst or psychotherapist the quotation makes the task of self-knowing sound much simpler than it really is. The individual who seeks a greater understanding and acceptance of himself or herself faces the long, arduous, humiliating and sometimes distressing task that Jung termed individuation, that is to say a coming to terms with oneself and achieving a greater measure of wholeness or integration. To surrender our defensive projections and prejudices is the task of a lifetime, an ideal never to be fully completed.

All this means that, in addition to our duty to God and to neighbours, we are faced with a third responsibility: our duty to the self within. This last is elusive. It is spurned by many Christians as smacking of self-centredness or narcissism. But this is a misunderstanding of how our relationship to our own self affects the way we react to other people spontaneously. 'How can I love my neighbour, if I do not love myself?'[8] asked Jung. (Here, too, we should understand loving as accepting, not romantic sentimentality.) This observation is confirmed by relationship-therapy, where it is not necessary to work with both parties to a relationship. When projection has lost some of its strength, the client or patient remarks 'Somehow he (or she) has been much nicer lately' or 'I don't know how it is, but people seem so much more friendly'.

In problems of relationship, therapy can help a vicious circle to reverse itself into a benign circle, help to restore balance and harmony, and help opposites to be productive and not destructive. As Jung recognized, this task is equally a religious and a psychological undertaking. All his own work, he said, was related to one theme: 'to penetrate into the secret of the personality.'[9] He saw the development of an individual personality as our essential responsibility and as the only true basis for a good relationship to other people. He saw this development as an ideal, not a goal. Each step towards wholeness is also an achievement of balance, integrity, union: loss of balance within the personality, resulting in exaggeration and internal disunity, is a sign of potential neurosis or mental illness. Perhaps the most dramatic example of this is schizophrenia or dissociation of the personality.

Jung believed that, to become a personality, it is crucial to assent consciously 'to the power of the inner voice . . . That is the great and liberating thing about any genuine personality: he voluntarily sacrifices himself to his vocation'.[10] To assent, however, is not to submit uncritically. The unconscious is an incomparable source of psychic energy. If we can heed it and consciously assent to its power we are in a position to use this energy according to our deliberate choice. This is the reverse of resigning ourselves to the unconscious and being ruled by it. The decisive factor, in Jung's view, is not morality (much of which is convention) but a sense of vocation. He described this as 'an irrational factor that destines a man to emancipate himself from the herd and its well-worn paths'.[11] This is hardly distinguishable from the Quaker concept of the inner voice (with allowance for the unQuakerly use of 'herd' to describe our fellow beings—really an anthropological, not an insulting use). 'Personality (he continued) is always a vocation and puts its trust in God ... Anyone with a vocation hears the voice of the inner man: he is *called*.'[12]

Even with the warning about submitting to the inner voice, this emphasis on following one's personal vocation must, I think, be accepted with reserve. There have been murderers who gave way to the unconscious to the extent that they felt called by God to kill. Most fanatics and zealots are equally convinced of the rightness of their calling. Delusions are often felt to be the voice of God by the deluded. Then any enormity is felt to be totally right. With such issues at stake it is hardly adequate to recommend assenting but not succumbing, without explanation.

One has to bear in mind Jung's insistence that the unconscious is a source of intense but morally-neutral psychic energy which is released by the clash of opposites. The essential safeguard is (as mentioned earlier) the midpoint between conscious and unconscious, which Jung termed the Self. It achieves the necessary balance and so enables us to make conscious moral choices. The important point here is whether our choices and decisions are made with the due acceptance of unconscious pressures or on the asumption that we are totally free of any such thing.

The Quaker way supports this mid-point Self through sharing with one another and submitting to the guidance of values felt to be eternal. The Meeting thus provides, so to speak, something to hold onto while the voice of our calling is heard and its implications are considered. Then a balance is found and we can progress with new energy.

Many normal people fight shy of the very idea of an unconscious and would far rather concentrate on our outward duty of caring for others. Jung bluntly challenged this understandable fear. Suppose I obey all Christian moral teaching yet still discover 'that I myself am the enemy who must be loved—what then?'[13] As Christians we 'condemn and rage against ourselves'.[14] Indeed, some feel they are obliged to do this. Christian self-hate is quite common. Sometimes it is kept out of awareness by assurances of forgiveness and that we have been redeemed by Christ himself. This is a device similar to healthy-mindedness. Sometimes inner feelings of unworthiness such as Jung refers to may be kept at bay through good works. But this all too often gives to the recipients a suspicion that they are somehow being used by a 'do-gooder'.

Another way by which we seek to protect ourselves from a feeling of inner unworthiness is to attribute all our innate goodness to the presence of God within us and to attribute our innate evil merely to the absence of that good, to our failure to recognize and respond to it. On this view, the vast mass of evil in the world is projected onto those who are not followers of Christ, to the evil ones, the enemy, to those who are not 'saved' as we are. Sometimes even fellow Christians are the receivers of these projections, and reciprocate them. Then inter-denominational violence, brutality or even war break out between them.

'The development of personality (wrote Jung) from the germ-state to full consciousness is at once a charisma and a curse', since it entails isolation from the 'undifferentiated and unconscious'[15] mass of mankind. The achievement of personality requires 'fidelity to the law of one's own being',[16] which he described as 'a loyal perseverence and confident hope; in short, an attitude such as a religious man should have towards God'.[17] He saw the achievement of personality (in this sense) as being deliverance from convention, not submission to it. And he would have us recognize the existence within all of us of a large unconscious measure of original good and original evil. Perhaps surprisingly for a psychologist and analyst, he endorsed the reality of original sin. 'We struggle blindly (he wrote) against the healing dogma of original sin, which is nevertheless so utterly true'.[18]

Most of us do not feel the demand of the inner voice or of our vocation in such compelling terms as these we have been considering. Nor are we all so confidently and consciously aware of the 'law of our being'. But most people, I think, know what it is to be half-consciously aware of some new path in life which we are inwardly prompted to follow, come what may. Others (particularly of course within our family) may have to bear a large burden if we act on the prompting. We have to be wary of claiming that our inner call comes from God and must therefore not be resisted. We may be mistaken. The burden others must bear or share from our decision must be put into the balance and time allowed for an equilibrium or compromise to be achieved.

Such balancing is a normal and continuous part of everyday life. We feel urged in one direction, someone else is urged another. We want, or like or need what conflicts with the needs, likes or wants of others. But with give-and-take these differences get settled, mostly without too much self-sacrifice or guilt. This sequence of balance and adjustment of potential conflict occurs in simple and in serious, far-reaching issues. Shall we go to Meeting or stay to help look after the baby or get the lunch? Shall we answer a call to uproot ourselves and go to Ireland or Africa, leaving dependents behind? We may feel called to demonstrate in ways that provoke violence or to risk prison for a good principle, abandoning all other responsibilities till we are released. We may feel called to say or do what will disturb or alienate others. To follow our own inner calling is important—but so are the implications for others when we act on it.

Such a list of choices and decisions could go on for pages and ages. It is remarkable how easily the great majority of them are settled. What exactly is this ability to compromise, adjust, find a new solution, achieve a balance of interest and concern with other people? Without it, we cannot advance towards personal wholeness, or answer our calling, but how does it arise? Much depends, of course, on our relationships with those who are also affected by what we decide. If relationships are good, the outcome is simple to reach. If they are bad, if may be impossible.

We need not pause here to consider these subtleties of relationship, except to note that the crucial factor is not so much the simple facts but the unconscious and emotional implications for all who are affected by them. Our present task is to regard in a more general way this question of following one's inner calling. We have to be ready to heed Jung's insistence on emancipating oneself from 'the herd' and from convention. This freedom will be affected by our membership of any religious organization or worshipping group. Our inner calling arises within that special context, since such membership provides us with its own accepted values. We live in several different psychological environments and each requires our loyalty, matching our own aims and aspirations with those of others collectively as well as individually. Each *milieu* has its own conventions, appropriate to different ways of life and social roles, to all of which we adapt ourselves as best we can.

In such a complex society as ours, these various conventions are useful. There are far too many of us for each of us to 'be ourselves' the whole time. It would be confusing for a policeman to behave like a clergyman or hospital nurse like an actress. We need to know what to expect of people according to their role. It upsets us if somebody acts too differently from the convention we know.

Most professions have unwritten but quite rigid requirements of manner, mannerism, behaviour and ethical standards. Sometimes one fits easily and naturally into the appropriate role. Then we speak of 'the born teacher' or 'the born nurse'. But if our job demands a role that is not natural to us, we must cultivate new ways. This may come easily to us or only after conscious effort and some mistakes.

Jung called this process of adaptation 'a collective necessity'.[19] But he recognized a risk in it. 'It is a stopgap and not an ideal, either in the moral or in the religious sense, for submission to it always means renouncing one's wholeness.'[20] The advantages are usually easier to see than the risk.

Difficulties will arise if we identify ourselves with our role and its conventions. We adopt what Jung called a *persona*. By derivation this Latin word means literally something through which sound passes. It was used for the mask which fitted over the whole of an actor's head in classical drama. The voice sounded from inside it, through the opening for the mouth, as used with powerful effect in Sir Peter Hall's modern production of the *Oresteia* of Aeschylus. Psychologically the persona masks the identity of the individual. It forms a kind of role-costume. It is adopted mainly unawares. But if we identify ourselves with it and assume it really is our natural personality, we shall be unable to do without it when we are in an inappropriate environment. We become like an actor who can never be off-stage or play an unfamiliar part. Jung believed that, with a little exaggeration, we can say 'that the persona is that which in reality we are not but which in our own and other people's opinion we are'.[21]

Identification with our persona results in rigidity and then it is maintained even when out of place. This makes others feel uncomfortable, as though in the presence of a robot, and a somewhat brittle and touchy robot. 'In favour of an ideal image (wrote Jung) into which one would prefer to mould oneself, too much that is generally human has to be sacrificed'.[22] This is specially liable to happen when the persona has been chosen to compensate some unacceptable aspect of the unconscious. For instance, someone who is vaguely and disturbingly aware of pressure from the shadow of a vicious tendency to cruelty or lust, may develop a rigid persona of exaggerated gentleness or puritanical chastity. This may result in taking a job in which kindness and goodwill are the necessary convention. Then the strain of living up to the convention may become intense. Some people find compensation in leisure activities that become more important than normal work which dwindles into an unrewarding routine. In these ways the collective necessity can become a personal handicap and provoke internal, emotional conflict.

Any movement, organization or community evolves its own accepted code of behaviour, scale of values, ways of speaking and tokens of membership. This is a strongly marked feature of religious and ideological organizations and it does much to mitigate the fear of loneliness or isolation in following the demands of one's inner individuality. It is a relief from this anxiety to join with like-minded people seeking a similar goal. We joyfully adopt their collective persona and feel secure as a member. We feel we have become accepted members of an elite. Hence the collective ecstasy characteristic of some charismatic and evangelical sects, to which susceptible people respond with ecstatic enthusiasm or even hysteria.

Those many people who are from time to time dogged by uncertainty and doubt about ultimate things are liable to envy this hypnotic loyalty and identification, where certainty reigns supreme and all questions are answerable. Jung invites us to look at the hidden side of all this, the unconscious opposite of these dramatic conversions. The rigid persona of those who are suddenly and dramatically 'saved' betokens an equally marked weakness in the unconscious. 'Inwardly (says Jung) they are as weak, malleable, and "soft-centred" as they are inflexible and unapproachable outwardly'.[23] Such people, for all their initial enthusiasm, are liable to become disenchanted and look around until they can find some equally enticing system of belief.

These features of the persona may not, at first glance, seem to have much relevance to the sober way of Quakers—not much given today to high-powered evangelism, preferring the restrained 'outreach' and wary of exaggerated enthusiasm and sudden conversion. Nevertheless we have our own collective persona that we normally take for granted. Our very simplicity is catching. Like any denomination or sect, we treasure our conventions, modest as they are. We, too, are wise to heed Jung's warning that the persona is a collective necessity but not a goal or ideal. He added that the 'personality can never develop unless the individual chooses his own way, consciously and with moral deliberation'.[24] There is, perhaps, no great risk of 'Quakerism' becoming a branch of theology at the expense of the personality-development of individual members, though some of our best theological brains may be tempted that way.

There is another risk that is commoner. This is the hampering of ministry by conventional attitudes. Perhaps, in our relative openness and informality, we are subject to conventional Quaker attitudes more than we realize. Conventions of manner and speech are no great matter and have their uses. But a convention of always seeing the bright side, being aware of only the beauty and goodness in life and (by association) in ourselves—these may stifle our inner stirrings to recognize another side to life and of ourselves. The anxiety of recognizing the reality of both sides produces a potentially creative tension that can release new energy and set us a little freer. If I read Jung's teaching aright, complacency might become a pitfall in our path, now that we are no longer persecuted but, on the contrary, inherit the goodwill our predecessors eventually secured.

In the pioneering, non-conformist years of revolt against religious artificiality, Quakers were cruelly persecuted. Their insight provoked the church establishment to the full fury of unconscious doubt disturbed. We are the comfortable and secure inheritors of these excesses and this courage. We are no longer a persecuted minority. Are we content to be the pensioners and beneficiaries of the puritan revolt, sitting quietly week by week testifying to the fundamental truth of a religion of acceptance and caring, in a world largely dominated by material envy and greed, violence, injustice, nationalism and hostile ideologies?

The challenge presented by the sober but relentless

impact of Jung's discoveries, his persistent telling us what we do not want to hear, offer a very different outlook for those who care enough. This is the challenge to look inwards and face what we see, to take our own individual plunge into the unknown side of ourselves, where the inner light beckons and points, where the presence of God is felt and where the evil cauldron bubbles.

Or shall we choose to conform to the gentle and kindly Quaker persona, not only in our Meetings (where it is a collective necessity) but in our lives, at every turn? The occupational risk of all who 'believe that they ought to believe' is to adopt a persona and then identify themselves with it, and so to delude themselves that all is well, and all is well, at least with us. This is an alluring temptation in present-day society so prone to substitute images for realities, where (as mentioned at the beginning of this book) most of our thinking tends to be visual, where we worry most about how things will look, not what they are, where only seeing is believing, where insight is mistrusted and pictures convince.

Some of us will choose one way, some another. The challenge that faces us is simply to recognize a choice and then to follow our individual calling with the guidance of those we trust.

10 Maleness and Femaleness

In the English translation of Jung's Collected Works there is a paper dated 1939 in which he wrote 'In the unconscious of every man there is hidden a feminine personality, and in that of every woman a masculine personality'[1]. This is still one of the most challenging and far-reaching of his ideas. It is as topical and controversial today as it was then, though in a different way. In this chapter we shall explore some of its implications for relationships, individually and in society.

At the time Jung's paper appeared all Europe faced the menace of Nazi and Fascist totalitarian tyranny and the psychic plague of total war. Jung's assertion must have struck any average man or women (who came across it) as irrelevant and fanciful or plain crazy. Sexual roles were much more rigid then than now, conventions were more distinct and taboos stricter. Demarcation lines between male and female were socially almost impassable through-out society. Any average man would probably have responded to Jung jocularly (such as 'Soon they'll be telling me I'm pregnant') and his wife with tolerant dismissal of an obvious absurdity ('Whatever will they think of next?'). And how about Quakers? My guess would be 'That is not an idea that would have occured to me'—nothing stronger than that, because traditionally Quakers have not been much troubled about status between sexes.

Jung had, as a matter of fact, put forward this idea (a little less starkly) some twenty years earlier: 'A very feminine woman has a masculine soul, and a very masculine man has a feminine soul'.[2] This concept was not accepted even by Freudians, who are perhaps the least easily shocked of all mankind. It was a revolutionary idea because of the certainty with which sexual roles were at that time accepted. After all, God (or Nature) had designed two sexes. They were there, clearly distinguishable, from birth.

Most occupations were then segregated as man's work or

woman's work, even in the home. All (but a very few) saw what fathers undertook and what mothers did, among friends and neighbours and in the home. Children were schooled into what boys should do and be like, and what girls should do and be like and also how each should behave towards the other. These differences were not just a question of manners but were strict stereotypes. A boy should be 'a proper boy' and a girl 'a real girl'. Everyone admired a manly man and a womanly woman and scorned the opposites. Girlishness in a boy or tom-boyishness in a girl were disturbing symptoms in the eyes of parents and teachers. Each sex should play with appropriate toys and, not swop over. Boys and men must not cry or knit. Girls and women should not shout or fight.

All such rules were obvious, natural, proper. There should be no inner taint or suggestion of the opposite sex in any of it. In this comprehensive sense of convention and taboos, sexual roles played an integral part in the developing persona of every child. This was so not only in obvious externals of dress and games and behaviour but in subtle traits of personality, in values, ideas, tastes: these too were distinguished as appropriate for a boy or a girl, a woman or a man. So also were mannerisms, tones of voice, choice of words, even food and especially drink.

These differences were not just niceties of any particular group or class (though these did exist also) but were essential features of society, even though details varied in different places. At the time Jung was writing, such rigid distinctions between the sexes were part of the real world, the collective persona of female and male. Male and female were natural opposites, like day and night, light and dark, friend or enemy. They were alternatives. Where should we be without them, without right or left, up or down, this or that? We tend to assess life through opposites. Depth psychology had not yet demonstrated publicly that there is a vital sense in which opposites are not alternatives but react to each other, relate to each other, complement each other and should, in the interest of wholeness and harmony, be kept in balance.

The Second World War brought about dramatic outward changes to many of these rigid conventions and assumptions, just as the previous world war had done. During the first war, women escaped from domestic life or domestic work into factories in their thousands and even millions or went onto the land as farm-workers not because of changing attitudes but because men were recruited and conscripted by the million to kill and be killed in trench warfare. In the second war, women were for the first time recruited into the fighting services, put on uniform and worked alongside men. Long-serving, professional officers faced the novel responsibility of maintaining good order and discipline in the face of the temptations of 'fraternization' between men and women under their command. To the surprise of many, the presence of ATS, WAAFS or WRENS on a service station raised morale and efficiency, especially in dangerous situations.

These outward changes in sexual stereotyping were forced on everyone by the total war and harsh struggle for survival. Both men and women mostly welcomed the presence of the other sex. There were some less obvious snags. Between the wars, Jung had observed 'A man regards it almost as a virtue to repress his feminine traits as much as possible'.[3] And he added that it was formerly regarded as unbecoming for a woman to be mannish. All the careful nurturing in the collective sexual stereotypes, in what was womanly or manly, suddenly seemed less relevant. Women found they could work as well as, or better than men, in work always assumed to be masculine. Men found they had no monopoly of courage, endurance, toughness in facing danger and hardship. Each found their own assumptions about the other sex to be less realistic than they had assumed. Women were not only domestically capable, men were not always tough, brave and heartless.

The new circumstances of total war inevitably changed the circumstances of almost everybody, whether they were combatants, objectors or in reserved occupations or too old or too young to be conscripted or too handicapped to be directed. The normal personas, the partly unconscious guises in which people had played their part in life, had to

125

be revised. The lucky ones found an opening to which their abilities and persona were appropriate and useful. The unlucky ones were unable to adapt themselves and were drafted to uncongenial work and situations they were unfitted for. Men, for instance, whose persona included heroism, relished the dangers of combat. Those whose persona included the skill and daring of a racing-driver, relished flying and some became aces. Men found they could be cooks, barmen, batmen, nurses, orderlies; women that they could drive cars and lorries, become skilled mechanics, interpreters, flight controllers or take up civilian occupations normally monopolized by men. As in normal, peace-time life, those whose persona and ability were appropriate to the available opportunities sometimes fitted-in so successfully that they identified themselves with the persona and so risked excessive and obsessive commitment and overwork. There were also many whose persona was rigid and unadaptable who became unsuccessful and awkward misfits.

These war years high-lighted Jung's teaching on the part played in work and in relationships by the persona (described in the last chapter). The readjustment to new conditions of work and living reoccurred in the return to peace. Roles and relationships again changed dramatically as they will over again if there are far-reaching social upheavals in the community.

There are the equivalents of these upheavals and changes in the life of individuals living in normal, stable times. These involve adaptation and readjustment, for instance on getting married, starting a family, after divorce, separation or bereavement, at retirement or redundancy and unemployment, or personal disablement or the mental illness of husband or wife, or birth of a handicapped child. All these demand changes of role, often changes of sexual role, and the creation of a new persona. Unlike the social changes we have been considering, however, these have an additional complication. This is the part played by the unconscious relationship between maleness and femaleness within each personality and between the two partners. The work of Jung and his associates and followers has much to show on this aspect of changing circumstances.

Among psychotherapists it is a commonplace that there are four partners to a marriage. Husband and wife each have a conscious and an unconscious side to the personality—a known and an unknown side. This is why superficial advice-giving and moral exhortation (however well-informed or authoritative) are of no avail when the partners are estranged. The unconscious aspects of their difficulty prevent their accepting advice or direction.

If there is an emotional estrangement between them it may centre around an apparently identifiable issue, like where to go for a holiday or how to divide the joint income or regulate their sex life. But such issues cannot be resolved by prescribed common-sense or give and take. People who are estranged are unable to compromise. Their mutual inner disharmony robs them of the ability to meet each other halfway or even discuss that particular topic without it ending in a quarrel or a grudging and resentful surrender. Deep-seated issues have an unfortunate way of spreading into other areas until the sad final stage of not being able to agree about anything and desperately seeking a way out.

Any attempt to understand (let alone influence) the relationship must start with understanding the two individuals, or at least understanding one of them. Whatever point of view one adopts (religious or any other), one is brought in the end to the balance between the way each sex sees the other and how differences that are discordant may become harmonious, whether there is to be peace or warfare between them or maybe an armed and envious neutrality. Anyone, from senior common-room to public bar, from Parliament, bench or pulpit or from nextdoor can say how men or women ought to treat the other sex. But until the partners can be helped to 'listen to their own nature' such views have no real influence on them.

Jung's contribution to this basic question of 'how' (rather than 'ought') takes the problem a stage farther. He discovered and demonstrated that the truly basic issue is not, so to speak, between man and woman but between masculinity and femininity within each partner. The whole intricate question involves working downwards from the social situation to the single individual and also working upwards from a psychological understanding of the individual to the widest implications of social role and religion. We will therefore consider Jung's contribution and then concern ourselves with the Quaker implications.

Jung regarded a full, stable and lasting relationship in marriage (or the equivalent) to be not only satisfying, enriching and a source of happiness. He called it 'a true and undeniable experience of divinity, the transcending power of which blots out and consumes everything individual'.[4] This view contrasts with popular ideas and formulas for running marriage successfully, as though such a complete relationship were no more complicated than a feat of cookery or an intricate game.

On the contrary, Jung's view confirms the experience of those many who find marriage a unique source of inner stability and growth, of meaning and enterprise and wholeness and delight. His reference to the 'experience of divinity' may accord well with what most people experience when they are in love, a truly transcending experience, not only an ecstatic pleasure. This contrasts with the regular Church view that marriage was ordained as a symbol of 'the mystical union that is betwixt Christ and his Church' and for 'the mutual society, help and comfort of the partners' and for 'the procreation of children' and also 'a remedy against sin, and to avoid fornication'[5]. Jung did not have a great deal to say about marriage in prescriptive terms. He was concerned with psychological differences between the two sexes, especially those that are unconscious for it is these which mainly determine the quality of the relationship. That is what concerns us here.

The balance of female and male sexuality is an ever-topical concern. Recently it has become a social, political and legal issue involving equal pay and sexual discrimination. In all these ways it is a subject of emotional intensity, sometimes of bitter antagonism among partisans. In all religious sects and denominations, sex relations are also of deep concern. In every marriage and 'marriage of true minds'[6] the same balance needs to be continually sought, maintained and restored. This takes place within the social and psychological context of the time and place, the conventions and taboos of behaviour, dress, ways of speech to which each individual makes some adjustment between obedience and rebellion, acceptance and defiance. When a full and dynamic harmony of maleness and femaleness can be achieved we reach perhaps the summit of well-being and wholeness. During periods of estrangement and discord, we experience the depths of misery if the relationship is one to which we are fully committed. This involves much more than a matching of the persona, stereotype and role of one partner with those of the other.

'Every man (wrote Jung) carries within himself an eternal image of woman, not the image of this or that definite woman, but rather a definite feminine image'.[7] And, of course, so does every woman carry within herself an archetypal image of masculinity, not just a father-image. These affect the formation of the persona and not vice versa. The persona is one's own constructed image of oneself (as one would like to be and comes to believe one is). These images are of the other sex and are of obscure origin, perhaps innate. They form what Jung called the soul-image, that is to say the godlike or goddesslike ideal latent in the unconscious. The persona is formed in contrast to the soul-image: one is the image of oneself, the other an image of the other sex.

Thus the soul-image plays an important part, albeit unconsciously, in how one sees oneself, one's tastes and ideals and the kind of part one seeks to play in life. External conditions and stereotypes also play a part in forming the persona, but no part in forming the soul-image. The soul-image comprises features common to myths and fairy tales. 'We meet these same motifs (wrote Jung) in the fantasies, dreams, deliria, and delusions of people living today. . . . They impress, influence, and fascinate us'.[8] We project our soul-image onto the lover, beloved or partner, as onto people we meet. This process is much in evidence during adolescence and during courting or being courted and of falling in love and being attracted. It often comes to the fore again in middle age but is perhaps never wholly inactive. Husbands and wives often recognize something of the soul-image of their partner ('Just your type, dear' or 'Hardly your type, I should have thought'). It is much less easily recognized in oneself. We are simply aware of a magnetic, mysterious attraction in some people, not in others. With men, the physical type of those who carry his soul-image is often the most easily recognized feature; with women it is something less obvious (at least to a male writer). With both of them physical, sexual attraction is not the whole explanation as some biological-minded authorities seem to believe. It is also, and chiefly, idealistic, expressed by Shelley (in a letter) as 'seeking in a mortal image the likeness of what is perhaps eternal'.[9]

In middle age especially, these projected images may be used against the partner if they are estranged and can no longer carry one another's soul-image and resent having it put upon them. Then the 'mortal image' appears in the guise of the fatal 'other man' or 'other woman', often very different from the partner and representing aspects of the soul-image the partner was not able to carry. These sad and sometimes tragic upheavals cry out for skilled therapy if they are to be surmounted constructively and not destructively.

In spite of the ever-increasing rate of divorce, most marriages cope with these crises and forge a relationship that is an intricate and subtle compound of the fourfold aspect of marriage and develop their own unique union of opposites which they recognize as We or Us. Once more we see the 'spark of opposites' that Jung identified as the source of vital, creative energy.

As is well-known today, Jung introduced the terms *animus* and *anima* into depth psychology. They merit some short explanation here to distinguish them from masculine or feminine aspects of the persona. The animus is the hidden, internal and unconscious side of a woman's personality as the anima is of a man's. The hidden masculine side of a woman is the reverse side of the feminine persona she presents to the world. Of a man, Jung says 'The persona, the ideal picture of the man as he should be, is inwardly compensated by feminine weakness'.[10] As so often happens, outward strength of one kind is balanced by an inner weakness. These inner compensating opposite characteristics explain the otherwise baffling instances of men and women who seem to be the very opposite at home from the person they are at work or in a social gathering. Saint at work, tyrant at home, for instance; masterful at work, sheepish at home (or vice versa).

Jung regarded thinking and feeling as opposite tendencies, as are (in his view) sensation and intuition. In any person, the more one of each pair is dominant, the more unconscious its opposite will be (and the reverse). He regards feeling as characteristic of women and thinking of men, the opposites being in the animus and anima respectively. Whereas (at least ideally) 'logic and objective reality commonly prevail in the outer attitude of man . . . in the case of woman it is feeling'.[11] He suggests that theorizing, categorizing and reasoning are masculine characteristics whereas emotional and subjective characteristics are feminine.

A man who hears a child cry may, for instance, start working out what the possible trouble may be: a woman comforts the child first. She is concerned with what makes people happy and unhappy, comfortable and uncomfortable in practice. With him there are theories and generalizations. Then there are the unconscious sides. A highly intelligent thinker and logician, the good abstract reasoner, may well be subject to unexpected moods and even childish tantrums when he gets home, quite the reverse of the calm assessment of abstractions and acute reasoning he shows at work. At home his anima has taken over.

Similarly a woman who is sensitive to how others feel and knows instantly how to deal with an emotional crisis and what will reassure or alarm, please or displease other people, may puzzle and irritate those at home by an outburst of impatient chop-logic, swash-buckling opinions based on nothing and uncontrollable argumentativeness from the animus who is having a field day. What comes forth from animus or anima is crude, spontaneous, uncontrolled, full of energy, morally neutral and entirely out of (conscious) character—moods or outbursts. Such occasions (and who has never known them?) call out a reaction from the partner, often from the anima or animus of the partner, and, like Tweedledum and Tweedledee, they will fight it out.

Such distressing and humiliating puzzles make good sense if one is aware of the fourfold relationship and of the way animus and anima balance the two personas. As most of us have experienced, such quarrels are peculiarly painful, baffling and upsetting. They are as unpremeditated as a sneeze and all we can do is to try to restrain their vehemence and then, when peace comes, try to understand what has been happening. The more the unconscious aspects of a quarrel can be recognized, the more fruitful will be the outcome and the more blissful the reconciliation.

Jung gives a somewhat unedifying account of this type of quarrel. It is given here as it clearly illustrates the way these tiresome but necessary things happen. 'No one can converse with an animus for five minutes (says Jung) without becoming the victim of his own anima'.[12] The result is 'commonplaces, misapplied truisms, clichés ... platitudes. .. vulgar abuse' in an all-too-common mixture. Referring to the animus that may erupt from a woman, Jung comments 'Unconscious assumptions or opinions are the worst enemies of woman; they can even grow into a downright demonic passion that irritates and disgusts men'.[13] This will energise the anima of her antagonist, taken over by feeling, as he blusters with fury or sulks in misery and dejection and mourns the (temporary) demise of his soul-image whom he deeply and truly loves. And his tantrums equally irritate and disgust her.

Jung characterized the wordy, theorizing way of men by using the ancient Greek term *logos* and the emotional, feeling way of women by *eros*. The former has been much used by theologians ('the Word was made flesh, and dwelt among us')[14] the latter relegated as an inferior partner to *agape* (or sexless love). Christians have notoriously kept a firm hold on the feminine and therefore on eros. And not only Christians. One might fairly say that Sex (in its modern sense, with a capital letter) has been the modern invention of men. Is it not men rather than women who theorise about Sex, make it into a technique concerned with the skilled manipulation of objects and tend to boast of their prowess (as though they were talking of athletics) and are so alarmed by the prospect of failure that many men are unsure of the difference between impotence and sterility?

In contrast, as Jung pointed out, 'For the woman the erotic principle has nothing whatever to do with "genital connections", or some such savoury formulae invented by the erotically blind masculine reason'.[15] Elsewhere he wrote 'To the woman the erotic relation is the only real and determining factor. To her marriage is a relationship with sexuality as an accompaniment'.[16] These two attitudes to the sexual relationship are opposite and, as usual therefore, may be the source of creative energy if they can be combined and not treated as alternatives. Indeed, their harmony is not merely symbolic of creation, it is literally and physically also the act of creation.

Jung was well aware of the dangers of a one-sided emphasis on the logos side of the psyche and the corresponding neglect of the eros side—a theoretical way of describing the cataclysmic dangers that threaten us 'from an unbalanced concentration of technical progress at the expense of humanity, of eros. It is mere foolishness to attribute this solely to the run-away dominance of men over women, as partisans are inclined to do. Both logos and eros are human characteristics. In men the logos is obvious and conscious, the eros unconscious in the anima. With women it is the other way around.

Thus, in Jung's view, the dangerous unbalance has to be restored by both sexes in harmony not in discord. But this is only possible to the extent that individual men and women are able to balance the two sides of their own personality, logos and eros, masculinity and femininity. The task (which Jung referred to as 'to build up a new civilization'[17]) must be begun internally by individuals, then they can work together. The tragedy is that we are so accustomed to seeing opposites as alternatives that we tend to see the sexes also as antagonistic and eros and logos as irreconcilable in 'the war of the sexes'.

PART THREE

Response

11 Harmonising Opposites

In this third section we shall consider the Quaker response to Jung's ideas and discoveries outlined in previous chapters.

That famous assertion of his about *knowing*, not just believing, neatly symbolizes the way both he and Quakers regard religion—not as theory, doctrine or dogma but as experience. His warning about psychological theorizing is paralleled by the traditional Quaker caution towards theology. Theories tend to be lifeless and routine in one's personal life, however valid in their own context. Jung's attitude towards theory matches the spirit of George Fox's witness: 'This I knew experimentally'[1] and matches also his celebrated challenge: 'But what canst thou say?'[2]

The old-style 'thou' (still cherished by some Friends for its grammatical accuracy) makes it clear that George Fox was speaking to the Ulverston congregation as individuals rather than collectively. He did not ask them as a body what their faith was or what their Church taught. He confronted each one, as we should say now, with 'But what do you say yourself?'. For Quakers then and now, responsibility rests firmly on each individual: response to new ideas (and to old ones) is not laid down in something called Quakerism, which is only a convenient name for the developing faith and practice of Friends. We need no 'imprimatur' or hierarchical approval, disapproval or censorship of new ideas. We are committed to using ('with discernment'[3]) our own judgment and 'leading', with the help of other Friends and Attenders. Even our Advices are not laid upon us 'as a rule or form to walk by'[4] but are subject to revision and discussion. What, then, *do* we say? No Friend would wish to reply for others, in response to Jung. But it is possible, without presumption, to distinguish between ways of responding.

First, there are the reactions of those who are familiar with analytical psychology as a theoretical system, elaborated by many followers of Jung. For them, it is a well-documented, comprehensive system, distinct from Freud's, but similarly emphasizing the fundamental significance of the unconscious (individual and collective) and the influence it has on relationships, behaviour and mental health. Some specialize in the therapeutic applications of Jung's psychology, others in its diagnostic uses or its relevance for anthropology, mythology, literature, mysticism and comparative religion. Others have a professional interest in its relevance for educational method, training in pastoral work, counselling and personal guidance. Yet others are concerned with his teaching from a philosophical point of view, particularly in relation to existentialism and psychosynthesis. All these may be regarded as vocational or functional uses of Jung's work and as forming a constructive part of the Quaker response in many spheres.

All such response demands intelligent and objective assessment of Jung's system of thought and contributes to its development: it is specialized and functionally relevant for a particular interest or occupation. In our present context it has to be contrasted with a radically different way of responding. We can best, perhaps, call this personal in the sense in which John Macmurray distinguished functional relationships from personal relationships.

A personal relationship is peculiar to individuals. It depends on feeling and on values inwardly held; it is emotional and subjective. In Quaker parlance we acknowledge our own personal responses when we say something 'speaks to our condition'. This well-worn phrase implies that something has a special relevance for us inwardly, has some effect on our way of seeing life and on our value judgments. We are stirred and concerned.

In professional and academic work, students are necessarily trained to keep the two kinds of response separate. Some people, of course, respond to Jung's ideas in both ways, objectively and subjectively. Others are not concerned with the functional response as part of their own vocational work but are intimately concerned with its bearing on their inner uncertainties, difficulties and their faith.

Another response may be termed popular or 'pop', in the sense of popular journalism or pop music or pop psychology. Ideas are presented for entertainment rather than serious use, usually briefly and often facetiously and with comic exaggeration and extravagance, over-statement and arresting novelty, with a sort of 'I ask you' manner of the presenter. This technique is skilfully exploited by entertainers and gains its attraction by contrasting opposite opinions in an amusing and unexpected way. Potentially serious (or even disturbing) issues may be raised and an audience or reader instantly tickled by quick repartee or with exaggeration and a brisk passing on to something else.

This method of amusing people has developed into an acceptable, cheerful social idiom that makes for easy, simple and reassuring jollity and some good laughs. It is a kind of collusive agreement that things are far too bad, complicated or difficult to be taken seriously. (Indeed, seriousness is the prime taboo.) It represents a funfair entertainment like dodge-'em cars, brisk and exciting and hilarious, colliding but not too dangerously, and spinning off for more hair-breadth narrow shaves. But there is a limit as no one wants a head-on collison so you must keep to the conventional way round.

Psychological ideas are often treated in this way, more in ordinary everyday life than in entertainment. The same taboo against seriousness provides us with a way of glancing at a serious issue but not taking it seriously, in which the unconscious becomes a sort of Shakespearean clown, nonsensical but with a potent undercurrent of meaning. Phrases like 'only in the mind', 'over-compensating', 'not sufficiently motivated' and terms like complex, obsession, manic are used in the same half-serious, jokey, dodge-'em car way. Unfortunately life cannot be all made into this type of entertainment and the misunderstanding of psychological events and brushing aside of symptoms of real distress can have tragic results, as when someone in urgent need of help is brushed-off as only trying to get attention, getting out of the chores, putting it on, or needing a kick in the pants.

Another response to psychological ideas is similar to this 'popular' one and sometimes occurs among students or trainees in psychology, counselling or social work. This is the use of technical terms to explain-away a difficultly that is somehow threatening or to classify a patient or client (whose need is not met by being pigeon-holed). To give a psychological assessment or diagnosis (especially in technical terms) can help one to feel in control of a fraught situation that raises challenging issues. For instance, a patient's or client's firm disagreement may be dismissed as 'resistance', his lateness as aggression, her gratitude as unconscious dependence or an attempt at seduction. Feelings of persecution may be written-off as being paranoia when someone actually is persecuted.

Anyone who is troublesome or difficult to understand may be labelled neurotic or manic-depressive or obsessional. The labelling may be correct according to the system of classification and may reassure the professional. But the client needs help. Classifying has its uses but to the distressed it may come as a rebuff and, to the classifier, be an emergency exit from responsibility to someone's need for understanding and insight, as may an exaggerated caution against the perils of involvement.

Our individual response to any of Jung's work, then, may excite our interest or disturb us. We may be enthusiastic about it or bored by it, be encouraged or outraged. We may acclaim it, idealize it, ignore it, or attack it. Why? There can, surely, be no other reason than because of the impact it makes upon us inwardly. The stronger our emotional reaction is, the more probable it is that we are unaware of the underlying significance that the issue has for us. It used to be said of Alfred Adler that, when confronted by a new patient full of anger, envy, resentment, anxiety or jealousy he would spontaneously draw up his chair like a fellow conspirator and say 'I do understand how you feel—but why do you feel it so strongly? Please tell me'. In a professional setting such an invitation some-times seems absurd: to the client or patient the reason is so obvious as to defy explanation. The exploration may then profitably begin.

How different this is from what so often happens in family life or between friends or at work, where the chief aim is usually to pour oil on troubled water (with sympa-thy or with disapproval) so that logic or common-sense may replace the awkward confusion of feeling. This natural response is, unfortunately, a snub to the underlying issues that are fuelling the strength of feeling and the distressed individual will sense being brushed-off, even when appre-ciating the sympathy. This sad result arises sometimes when someone of genuine kindness tries to comfort one for whom comfort is irrelevant. There is no substitute for insight.

When strong inner feelings are unexpectedly aroused in these ways (often to our own surprise) by issues that dis-turb us, our reactions are really defences against inner emotional pressure. It is sometimes clear how somebody else resorts unawares to such self-protection, for instance by fiercely-held opinions held dogmatically, by argumen-tativeness, exaggerated prejudice, repetitive beliefs and by anxiety or outbursts of hostility. But (as with Adler's patient) it is extremely difficult to recognize the same defensiveness in oneself—that what is psychological sauce for a goose is much the same for the gander. These are not matters of decision or logic or reasonableness. Indeed they interfere and annul reasonable discussion. They represent some turmoil or conflict of feeling, not of rational thought and they are apt to arise without warning whenever some issue arises that sparks-off inner feelings of aggression or anxiety, fight or flight.

Such events often seem ridiculous to an outsider or onlooker who is not touched in the same way and who, of course, can have no knowledge of their subjective signifi-cance, although the fact that someone is upset is obvious. Naturally, the stronger the turmoil of inner feeling, the more difficult it becomes to solve anything reasonably. Hence the well-known advice to cool it, sleep on it or talk it over with anyone who is not involved and can tolerate another person's strong feelings. The risks in these tiresome upsets are all too clear: we may act rashly or stupidly or even disastrously, hurtfully or shamefully.

Sometimes we are unable to act or decide at all but dither with increasing indecision and anxiety or anger, to the exasperation of those around us. Like the little gymnast walking the upturned beam mentioned earlier, we are for the time being in a perilous state of instability, trying to regain our balance so that we can get on with our task. This painful state of affairs may arise in any area of daily experience, in small issues or large ones, and in our relations to family, colleagues, friends or rivals, to authorities or dependents. Our human consciousness gives us the power of judgment and of foreseeing and imagining the results of our actions and therefore we are always and everywhere liable to conflicting feelings and values. When we find there is one such conflict that persists and which we cannot resolve we may develop a neurosis, or a malady that is the outcome of inner turmoil.

Fortunately, the majority of us are well-enough balanced most of the time to cope with a huge proportion of the minor conflicts and anxieties of modern life that keep popping out at us all through the day and sometimes at night too, in our dreams. Nevertheless, all but the luckiest among us have some sore spots in our personality, quirks of touchiness, thin-skinned sensitivities, as well as a few more deep-seated dreads and animosities that may cloud our judgment and disturb our peace of mind.

The satisfactory management of our life and our relationships largely depends on how we succeed in harmonizing the emotional impact of circumstances with our inner feelings, values and most cherished opinions. This harmonizing of inner and outer is what we colloquially call coping with life or with a situation. Both religion and dynamic psychology are deeply concerned with this ability to reconcile conflicting feelings and purposes, likes and dislikes, ideals and values. It can yield the creative outcome of a clash of opposites and is fundamental to individuation and personal well-being.

The religious attitude to life gives to this universal task a sense of vocation, a calling and the inner certainty of an ultimate ideal towards which we make our uncertain and faltering progress and it gives us a sense of direction. Our pilgrim's progress towards wholeness, unity and harmony is one version of the Quaker Way and is also the general meaning of what Jung meant by individuation. The contribution of depth psychology (stemming from Freud) is to throw new light on the paramount importance of unconscious factors and hindrances to the natural process of inner growth and so help us to regain our balance and come to terms with our frailties of personality.

The psychotherapist faces a task of formidable delicacy. She (or he) cannot impose the process of individuation or ensure growth by any technique. Since (by definition) the unconscious, personal shadow is made up of urges, aims, drives, and fears that are too threatening to be tolerated in consciousness and so have been repressed, both therapist and patient are working in the dark, exploring a secret territory. Should the therapist try too hard to uncover what lies hidden she will only meet with panic-stricken or hostile defences: if she does not try at all, nothing of any significance will come from the encounter.

Fortunately, the drive to repress unacceptable aspects of ourselves has its own opposite counterpart. This is the inherent urge towards wholeness, growth, harmony and individuation. This can be relied upon, as a physician and a nurse rely on the inherent recuperative urge of the patient's body towards its own kind of wholeness. Initially, the psychotherapist usr .ily has to contend with the patient or client's certainty that all his difficulties and problems stem from outside, from other people or from circumstances. The superstitious dread of the unaccepted parts of our own personality (which amounts to a dread of being unlovable) makes self-awareness, even in the most modest degree, a demanding task and a courageous achievement. Our spontaneous defences rally to its obstruction.

'It is my belief (said Joseph Conrad's character Marlow, in his compelling novel on the Ancient Mariner theme of intolerable inward guilt)—'It is my belief no man ever understands his own artful dodges to escape from the grim shadow of self-knowledge'.[5] Perhaps today one may presume to prefer 'self-awareness' to 'self-knowledge' and substitute 'person' for 'man'. We sometimes notice these artful dodges in other people, but in ourselves—oh dear, no.

It may be that some of Jung's ideas arouse a strong response in any one of us, perhaps on the fundamental relevance of the personal unconscious. Many people fervently deny its reality in anybody, most of all in themselves. And there seems no limit to the devices that serve to screen us (to our own impoverishment) from its existence. No one can persuade us then, of its significance. We have to experience that for ourselves.

If it is indeed (as Jung maintained) the province of religion and psychology to work together in helping individuals towards integration, balance and wholeness, is there anything that can be done within the ordinary Quaker context to help members of the Meeting? Advices, inspirational reading, theology and the arts can all help in different ways to clarify the task and to encourage us to undertake it, though they cannot do much towards a direct harmonising of one's personal shadow with one's conscious ideals and aims. Competent pastoral counselling by trained counsellors can be helpful in this task, still more can psychotherapy with one who has himself or herself qualified to undertake the work by personal experience of analytical therapy.

These aids are, however, seldom readily accessible and are inevitably expensive. Ambitious high-pressure group techniques, open to all comers, can be risky and should be approached with caution and after responsible enquiry. In the hands of inadequately trained leaders they can be harmful. In Chapter 14 of this book there is an outline of a simple venture that has been tried among members of a Quaker Meeting with modest success. It can be repeated without much difficulty or risk within a Quaker context. The booklist will also, it is hoped, be useful as an introduction or accompaniment to such a group.

To return to Jung's ideas and our Quaker response, we may now ask in a little more detail how we respond, individually and as a group, to the shadow, to the persona, the animus and anima, to introversion and extraversion in relation to ourselves. Most of these opposites can be responded to in the ways outlined earlier in this chapter, that is to say by subterfuges that help us to evade self-awareness. But we may reflect that, for instance, the personal unconscious is balanced by the familiar conscious self, for which Freud used the term Ego (a word often today used colloquially to mean self-esteem, and therefore not used here). We are all apt to regard the 'I' as being the 'real me' and all there is of personality within us.

We are thus liable to cold-shoulder the unconscious and keep it out of sight below the stage, like the ghost in Hamlet. Jung counsels us to try a different approach, to keep an open mind so far as we can and seek to make friends with that shadowy figure within and listen to what it tries to tell us—an encounter that is liable to be full of vitality that can energise us wonderfully as it surprises or discomposes us with its clash of opposites and its moral neutrality. It may shock and inspire us and lighten our darkness. Then, in our turn, we can exclaim 'Well said, old mole! Canst work i' the dark so fast?'[6] Each such encounter is a step in the direction of wholeness and we shall learn to find a friend where we feared an enemy.

The persona, too, has an opposite, which is the natural self. If the persona is cultivated knowingly, it can help us to fit-in and co-operate. But if it arises as an automatic defence against unacceptable aspects of the self we start to identify ourselves with it, as described earlier. The resulting denial of our own integrity results in conflict and tension internally. A child may face a similar difficulty. Take for instance an innately extraverted, active and aggressive girl born into a strictly non-violent, peace-loving, introverted Quaker family (a marriage of unison). The child cannot avoid developing a persona that is the very reverse of her innate personality, for a young child cannot rebel against both parents. The rigidity of the parents' meek and kindly joint persona leaves the girl in an internal and potentially unstable state of denial of the constructive and life-enhancing aspects of her personality.

The situation would be no easier for a boy in the same family. Indeed, if both parents were strongly inclined to associate violence with male aggression, then the problem might be even more severe for him. What all this amounts to is the simple proposition mentioned earlier, namely that harmony between opposites is the secret of individuation. If the parents, in our example, were able to face and not repress their own occasional aggressiveness, they could still support peace and non-violence but would not be alarmed by signs of aggression in daughter or son and could help the child to make good, constructive (and ultimately peaceful) use of aggression which, in one form or another, is after all essential for living. But if they are unable to do this their child's outbursts and energy will feel like a threat and their disapproval can only result in either rebellion (probably in adolescence) or an unreal, compliant defeatism.

It seems to be a law of psychological health and growth that morality should be based on accepting opposites (that is to say, on love) and not on repressing one of them. There is for Christians the prototype of this in the temptation of Jesus in the desert, when he faced squarely the urge to worldly success and power and chose love instead. For Buddhists there is the comparable drama of the Buddha's temptation by Mara (the personification of evil and tempter of mankind).

If we are accustomed to the prevalent Western way of seeing opposites as alternatives (one good, the other evil), we may interpret the temptation of Jesus and that of the Buddha as the reverse of this acceptance of opposites. We may object 'Both of them utterly rejected their tempter, far from accepting them as you seem to suggest. "Get thee hence, Satan"[7] is rejection, not acceptance'. This objection arises from a misunderstanding of 'accept'. In psychology accept does not mean agree with, go along with, put into practice. It means face up to, recognize and acknowledge in oneself. It is the reverse of denial, looking the other way, not seeing or acknowledging, as when we strive to suppress an unwelcome or shameful feeling for the sake of the persona, or when we automatically banish it from awareness (that is to say, repress it).

From a psychological point of view, Satan and Mara are each a personification of evil, the necessary and inevitable counterpart of good. This entered the mind both of Jesus and the Buddha in the same way that such archetypes appear to us in dreams. Each responded by recognizing (accepting) the claim of evil within and then consciously and courageously rejected it as a way of life. Each story thus becomes a charismatic and potent myth, radically different from the two-dimensional interpretation that evil is an external tempter like the wicked villain in a child's pantomime to be banished once and for all, so we can all sleep soundly, and the hero triumphs.

Evil is not wholly outside but also within us. We try to get rid of it by projection. But it is part of our humanity. If we are to deal with it we must first accept it as real and present within us, in the same way as the doctrine of original sin proclaimed. That was Jung's view. So far as temptation enters the picture, we are tempted by something only if part of us wants to accept it. Morality comes into it only when we know what is happening and decide what to do.

Of all the pairs of opposites portrayed by Jung, introvert and extravert are perhaps the clearest and best known. He made the distinction at some length and today the terms are familiar though they are often valued differently from the way he valued them. If we see them as alternatives, we ask ourselves 'Which am I?'. It is more realistic to think of introversion and extraversion as tendencies rather than categories of personality. Not only are there degrees in the scale between the two extremes but each 'extravert' has an unconscious introverted side (and vice versa).

For many people this is an unacceptable notion because we cannot see our shadow side. Our unconscious cannot be also conscious. One of the surprises that psychotherapy can bring is the discovery of this other side, that there is a potent inner side which is the opposite of the qualities we regard as obviously our chief characteristics. The therapist does not force this discovery upon the patient but helps, supports and prompts the patient to discover what is there already, lying unrecognized. With skilled help this gain in personal freedom and autonomy may be reached through dreams, phantasies and tastes as well as through memories and worries. For instance, a strongly introverted person develops a love of reading Whodunnits or watching boxing or dreams of haranguing a crowd; or a bold and worldly tycoon nourishes a love of science fiction, Wagner's music or abstract art or has Robinson Crusoe phantasies. If we are unable to balance our own psyche consciously and from choice, our unconscious side will do it, often to our embarrassment, sometimes to our delight.

Our present circumstances and past experience have an influence on this balance between introversion and extraversion. So do our persona and our inborn nature. Sometimes we impose an artifical balance and so do violence to our true personality. This is specially liable to happen when we cultivate too rigid a persona that does not really fit us. Then we have to silence the 'old mole' under the floor boards. But it will have its say somehow, sometimes with dramatic effect, as when a good clergyman's wife runs off with a driving instructor or milkman or when a sober scholar falls hopelessly in love with a young dancer or pop singer he has never spoken to.

One might think the Quaker way would be peopled mainly by introverted men and women, because of the silent stillness and meditative character of Meeting for Worship. But there is plenty of scope for extraversion. Most Quakers mix and chatter freely before and after meeting and are notoriously busy in outward activities, entertainments, demonstrations and the like. This helps members to find their own balance between extraversion and its opposite and perhaps also accounts for the sense of release and freedom that attenders and new members often experience. It also helps even weighty and seasoned Quakers whose life reaches a confusing phase of psychic change. This may happen at any time, though (as Jung pointed out) it is characteristic of middle age when even the most extraverted person may turn inwards towards spiritual, aesthetic, romantic and imaginative interests and values and concerns.

Less frequently, the turning at middle age may be out-wards and a hitherto introverted woman or man becomes more sociable, practical, objective—active and adventurous, to the astonished admiration of family and friends. In this latter instance, such a person may yearn for a quite different form of worship. Then they sometimes resign from membership or stay away from Meeting and devote themselves to outer and active ventures. These upheavals may enrich individuals and also the Meeting they belong to, provided the psychic change-of-life has occurred in the normal process of personal growth and individuation. Then a new and constructive stability is born from a new balance, not once for all but repeatedly.

Among public figures, the writer J. B. Priestley provides a vivid and dramatic example of this reversal and a new balance achieved in middle life. Few novels can be more typically extraverted than his *The Good Companions* and his *Angel Pavement*. Then followed his interest in the Time theory of J. W. Dunne (author of *An Experiment with Time* and also *The Serial Universe*) and Priestley's own Time plays and his fine *Literature and Western Man*, influenced (as Margaret Drabble points out)[8] by Jung. For such a metamorphosis to come about so creatively, there has to be a readiness to listen to the inner self and the courage to integrate its urges. The stability and support of a Meeting and the values acknowledged within it can wonderfully help this new stage of personal growth even in the modest changes that confront most of us. When the temporary stage of inner and outer adjustment is too disturbing or critical, the skilled help of a qualified counsellor or therapist can be instrumental in achieving a new balance. Such a person acts as a reliable friend and as a kind of communications satellite, relaying messages between the conscious and the unconscious. This is the function that Jung described as teaching people to listen to their own nature.

Sometimes we suddenly find a 'soul-mate' who seems to represent all that we most admire. Our two personas 'click' and we get locked into an unconscious partnership. We see eye to eye, strive for the same goals, fear the same perils. This is a partnership of unison or sameness, not of harmony. It is overwhelming and ecstatic and resembles falling in love although it is not necessarily sexual in any overt way. It is exhilarating because it feels like proof that our persona is real and is reflected back to us from the beloved. Analysts refer to this common experience as collusion. One needs to bear in mind that in psychological use it does not refer to a deliberate and thought-out stratagem. It is neither deliberate nor in essence conscious. The joyous feeling is its effect, screening us from the true inner situation.

When a Quaker attender applies for membership and talks over the possibility with two or more members, this collusive factor may arise in the form of an exaggerated over-enthusiasm. The applicant may feel that all problems will be solved by joining and all doubts made plain by 'Quakerism'. Those who join any religious or ideological sect on such a wave of enthusiasm are often liable to drop out again when some other identification comes their way. That is why such enthusiasts are normally asked to wait a little longer before applying. Such an applicant may be discouraged by this, and ruefully contrast it with the evangelical eagerness of some denominations and feel somewhat unwelcome. But experience has shown the wisdom of letting the pendulum swing before (rather than after) joining.

As previously noted, Jung classified personality into two pairs of opposite types, according to the predominant function. One pair is thinking and feeling; the other being intuition and sensation. In our present context the first pair is by far the more important. Each of the four functions can be either introverted or extraverted: thus Jung and his followers distinguish eight personality types.

We now return to the contrast (introduced in the previous chapter) between a thinking and a feeling attitude towards sexuality. To people of a thinking type, Sex is a subject to be studied intelligently and duly practised as a technique or as an intricate and elaborate game with its own 'rules' and specialised technical terms.

By contrast, people of a feeling type find such an approach unacceptable or even disgusting. To them, sex is a way of expressing emotion, not a topic or technique. It expresses emotional warmth, desire, spontaneity, involving closeness and play. Such differences of attitude may lead to sexual estrangement and personal disharmony, always puzzling, sometimes bitter, resentful and even violent. Neither is wrong but, if rigidly maintained, each provokes the other. People whose sexual attitude is balanced and adaptable learn to harmonise their sexuality through affection. As with other opposites, head and heart can be complementary, both within and between each partner. Such an achievement (sometimes hard won) is the mainspring of a happy, dynamic, stable and lasting sexual relationship. We can love other people without being sexually attracted and we can be sexually attracted without loving. But a fruitful and rewarding relationship is based on a mutual and affectionate harmony of differences.

It is psychologically naïve to suppose that sexual disharmony can be resolved by technical sex instruction alone. This over-simplification (which is not rare) is another instance of the contemporary preponderance of logos over eros in Western society. It is naturally resented bitterly by those who see it as masculine exploitation of women. A woman may be both repelled and attracted by the cerebral and somewhat impersonal and functional attitude of most men, the conscious attitude being compensated in the unconscious. This subtle interplay between both sexes is sometimes overlooked by feminists who regard loveless sex as nothing but exploitation of women and are blind to the corresponding exploitation of men by sexual provocation (sometimes conscious, sometimes unconscious).

Perhaps this bias is merely a passing phase, a swing of the pendulum, a reaction from the undeniable sexist repression of women that provoked it. Fortunately, in spite of such sad rivalry, men and women still succeed in harmonising logos and eros in their sexual differences, to their mutual delight and fulfilment. Perhaps some day there will be a publication under the title 'Towards a Quaker View of Love' to complement the popular and successful one about sex. Both are needed.

This is no frivolous suggestion. Something of the sort is surely overdue. The Puritan tradition behind the Quaker way has always been orientated towards logos and rectitude rather than love, sex and affection. Kindness, Compassion, Love do not appear in the index of *Christian Faith and Practice*. Even Sex occurs only in connection with the education of children and public morality. Sin comes nine times. The tradition relied on strict morality and convention to keep feelings at bay. If anything could be abused or over-indulged, abstention became the rule as, among many people, it still is. It does not, apparently, enter the Puritan mind that happy, well-adjusted, balanced personalities do not habitually over-indulge themselves or that kindness, goodwill, affection and creativity do not need rules and prohibitions. Love need not be schooled by regulations. Jesus showed a more tolerant attitude. He outraged the righteous and the sanctimonious by the company he kept. He reviled and threatened those who had a bureaucratic, legalistic or Pharisaical attitude, life-denying, moralistic and humourless. It is not always understood that strict suppression of feelings encourages revolt, thus leading to a vicious spiral.

The ability to accept the unconscious and the part it plays in life is basic to self-awareness. If we are aware that things go on within ourselves that are not rational and not wholly controllable, that sometimes we feel 'I was not myself' or 'I lost control' or if things sometimes grip us unaccountably and intensely (a person, a work of art, an event, a dream, a conviction) in a way that is positive and life-enhancing and full of meaning—then we have indeed been in touch with the unconscious.

We need also to accept that daily living, our tastes, values and certainties are not wholly products of reasonable thought and clear decision but of irrational feeling also. For better or worse, many of our actions and choices arise from mood and emotion rather than from thinking. To those many people whose predominant function is thinking, this suggestion may seem absurd and untenable, until they are forced by events to find it valid. By 'events' is meant not only what happens to them from outward circumstances but also from their inner emotional reactions. These may astonish them, being the opposite of how they usually react, so that they think 'What on earth came over me?'. If we do feel the impact of such happenings, then we can learn to accept this strange unfamiliar area of discovery and personal growth.

For many people this is a courageous enterprise. We are tempted to resist the challenge and keep going in the old way. But then some inner prompting calls us to the adventure of discovery. Myths, fairy-tales of bold young heroes, of tower-imprisoned or sleeping princesses or a chore-ridden youngest child—these may give us heart for their adult equivalents and the quest of that 'grail' that lures us on.

For all our cautious sobriety, Quakers have acknowledged the force of religious vocation—that which calls and beckons and inspires one to bestir oneself and take a risk. For some, the venture is outward and practical, for others (especially the middle-aged) it is an inward venture, demanding a continuous harmonising of opposites. In whatever terms we accept the challenge, it is fundamentally religious and recognizes an entity greater and more important than self-interest. It is both the means and the justification for the effort and it is a task that is never completed.

12 Vocation and the Collective Unconscious

The process that Jung called Individuation is the synthesizing of different aspects of the psyche into a whole. It is the means by which we achieve harmony within ourselves and become less defensive in our relationships with others. The more integrated we become, the less we project our own unacknowledged prejudices, motives and tendencies onto others and blame them for our own shortcomings. Through individuation the personality develops towards its own unique maturity. As adults we are apt to think we have 'put away childish things'[1] without realizing that some of the child lives on in us in the way we lead our lives and in the way we relate to people.

Maturity, independence, uniqueness comprise the goal of psychological growth. Individuation is the way we approach that goal. It is not a mere tranquillizer but a formidable achievement, similar to reaching a reconciliation with a long-standing adversary whom we would rather avoid or ignore. It is often even harder than that, since we do not even know exactly who the adversary is because it is hidden in the dark side of oneself. We come gradually and sometimes painfully to accept it and so live more at peace with ourselves.

This is the natural process of psychic growth. It depends on our ability to accept opposites and bring them into harmony. Identifying opposites helps us to recognize their influence but does not necessarily harmonize them. We have to experience them and learn to live with them if we are to bring them into balance. For instance, if a man is thrown into a dejected, sulky and hostile mood by somebody or if a woman is provoked into argumentative and hair-splitting arrogance of opinion, neither of them will be helped by being told that it is the anima or the animus making itself felt. They can only reply So what? But if each

155

knows about these inner presences and can recognize them, it becomes much easier to stop putting all blame onto the other party. All of us know, I think, what it means to experience an emotional upset or personal crisis and come out of it enriched, perhaps after a quarrel or some misunderstanding. In the appropriate legal phrase, the balance of our mind was disturbed and it is a pleasurable achievement to regain it. The prime incentive for this lifelong process is a sense of inner vocation, to which Jung attached such importance. The one who heeds it (at whatever personal cost) has an unmistakable aura of inner security and strength. All this has been touched on in previous chapters. It is summarized here to help clarify another issue that can easily be confused with it.

The collective unconscious is perhaps the most original and far-reaching of Jung's discoveries. It is distinct from the personal unconscious though it also plays a vital part in psychological growth and in our attitude towards transcendence. The shadow arises from repression but the collective unconscious is innate, a part of our psychological inheritance. Jung believed it arises from subjective experiences of human beings down the ages and is a kind of inner mythology that influences the way we think and feel. It emerges in dreams and imaginings, myths and legends, in images and archetypes which have a special and fascinating influence on how we feel and act and on our inner calling.

Jung insisted that vocation is not limited to the great liberators of mankind, to reformers, geniuses, saints, scientists or artists, but can come the way of anyone. There are times when we have a sudden and certain glimpse of the path we must take; we know it is right for us though we cannot say why. We feel it is what we must do, that it is our 'thing'. Sometimes to follow it means flying in the face of convention or common-sense or prudence—heartened by the Advice to 'live adventurously'.[2] It may be difficult to free oneself from the fetters of routine and convention and may entail some sacrifice. But we know it has got to be followed. Jung referred to 'the great and liberating thing

156

about any genuine personality: he voluntarily sacrifices himself to his vocation'.[3] He regarded the inhibiting pressure of convention as a serious bar to individuation. He wrote that submission to convention 'always means renouncing one's wholeness and running away from the final consequences of one's own being'.[4] Nevertheless, he accepted convention as a collective necessity. 'It is a stopgap and not an ideal, either in the moral or in the religious sense'.[5] The fact that conventions flourish is (he believed) proof that most of us prefer to follow a collective way than our own individual calling.

Unhappily, convention reinforces unconsciousness (saves one thinking and deciding). It becomes both cause and result of neglecting our unique path towards wholeness and integration. 'Collective man (wrote Jung) is threatening to suffocate the individual, the very individual who is absolutely indispensable'.[6] He was writing fifty years ago. Even so, one can hardly doubt the same is true today. Such thoughts do not make cheerful reading, especially to anyone who believes that human progress rests on political, economic and social change and not on the progress of each individual. 'The levelling down of humanity into a herd (wrote Jung) . . . must inevitably lead sooner or later to catastrophe . . . and the yearning to be led is inevitable.'[7] There is no lack of people eager for power in the sincere illusion that they or their party know what is best for society.

Jung had, of course, witnessed the headlong rise of Fascism and Nazism, the euphoric surrender of power and authority to the fatal charismatic leader and the surrender of individual judgment and moral responsibility to the Party by all except a few heroic resisters. He knew the terrible fate that these people suffered. Twelve years after the bitter experience of Nazism and Fascism, Jung commented 'one would think that the world had seen more than enough of what a well-disciplined mob can do in the hands of a single madman.'[8] He believed that to think in collective terms of vast organizations is dangerously shortsighted.

It is tempting today to think Jung's warning is exaggerated. But we have only to reflect on recent events to see the danger inherent in collectivity—sectarian conflict, football violence, inner-city rioting and violence, race riots, large-scale financial corruption, anti-police violence, outbursts of irrationality in political electioneering. 'All human control comes to an end (wrote Jung) when the individual is caught in a mass movement'.[9]

There is a dangerous tendency in Western societies for people to combine in masses around over-simplified and intensely emotional issues. All too easily a group or crowd or mob is liable to explode into violence collectively. In the name of democracy we come to rely on sheer numbers, not on reason or intelligence, seeking ever-larger organizations and majorities. This inevitably leads to 'the tremendous heaping up and accentuation of all that is primitive in man and the unavoidable disintegration of his individuality.'[10] The larger the group, the greater the disintegration of personality into its most primitive elements, the collective unconscious.

The result is all too familiar today, as we may witness on our television screens. The formation of a crowd lowers the moral and intellectual level of the members. Normally reasonable and friendly people become capable of any kind of excess that none of them would commit alone. Within a crowd 'psychic activity runs on in it like an uncontrolled law of nature . . . that comes to a stop only in catastrophe'.[11]

Jung criticized the contemporary view in society that only numbers have real meaning and considered the psychological effect: 'It thrusts aside the individual in favour of anonymous units that pile up into mass formations'.[12] State policy is then substituted for the moral responsibility of individuals. And the State, he explained, is not capable of happiness and contentment and an understanding of the meaningfulness of life, for it 'is nothing but a convention agreed to by independent individuals and . . . continually threatens to paralyse and suppress the individual'.[13] Then there breaks out 'a psychic epidemic': 'At any moment millions of human beings may be smitten with a new madness . . . another world war or devastating revolution'.[14]

In face of all this, spirituality might seem an irrelevant luxury, as we sit in our quiet little Meetings and thank God violence has not as yet reached our doors and we are not persecuted as the early Quakers were. We may take heart from the very one who made all these observations: 'Spirituality (wrote Jung) is never superfluous; it is a rare and inestimable treasure'.[15]

What would happen if our own massive Quaker Yearly Meetings neglected the well-planned and organized foundation of this very quality, spirituality? If we were to mistake collective zeal for the leading of the Holy Spirit or the voice of God, our Yearly Meetings would degenerate into a secular and political forum for partisan pressure groups and factions bent on power. Jung believed that a similar fate had already overtaken some of the Churches. They do not seem to know, he thought, 'the elementary axiom of mass psychology that the individual becomes morally and spiritually inferior in the mass'.[16] He believed Church leaders all-too-readily succumb to the popular faith in collective action and collective ideology instead of fulfilling their historic role of proclaiming that 'the salvation of the world consists in the salvation of the individual soul'.[17]

The feature of Western society high-lighted by Jung in these ways must, I think, affect any reader, but affect each one in an individual, characteristic way. This is bound to be so with most of his views, since he was concerned with the subjective view of life and that is unique to each one (and to himself, too). Inevitably we all see the world and one another in our own way, through our own lenses (so to speak), rose-tinted, yellow-tinted, dark-glassed or even polarized to take out glare. But mob violence is so vivid and menacing and so topical a psychic epidemic (in his apt phrase) that it arrests our attention and provokes our own response.

Fifty years ago Jung warned of these dangers of unbridled collective emotionalism and today we see how right he was. For peace-loving Quakers with their traditional belief in non-violence, these outbreaks are specially disturbing. Faithfully practising and preaching non-violence, resolutely demonstrating our witness for peace, we have to accept that these efforts make little impact on those many people who accept defensive violence as a regrettable necessity. Many, perhaps most, accept the pacifist ideal but not as an absolute. It has also to be accepted that large collective demonstrations are always in danger of getting out of hand, when the collective unconscious and frustrated aggression may lead to mindless violence, sometimes of manic proportions.

Jung constantly and consistently warned anyone who would listen of the terrifying dangers of collectivism and the vital importance of the individual and the personal inner vocation. The sad fact is, as the young Shelley proclaimed, that neither love nor reason is effective against collective violence.

> Men must reap the things they sow,
> Force from force must ever flow,
> Or worse; but 'tis a bitter woe
> That love or reason cannot change
> The despot's rage, the slave's revenge.[18]

Today we seldom think in terms of tyrants or slaves, except symbolically. But it is easy to recognize their modern equivalents. Perhaps we Quakers could evolve new kinds of Peace Testimony, for industrial, professional or communal peace and the renunciation of all violence and withholding of care. And yet maybe aggression is more a symptom than a psychic disease and we would do well to try to understand ever more fully the source and development of goodwill, compassion and affection. Demonstrations make little impact except on those susceptible to collectivism, any more than good sense makes much impression on those who are swayed by suggestion. When both love and reason fail to help, we can only search for other sources of goodwill.

In order to clarify the response of Quakers to Jung's observations it is perhaps simplest to imagine some possible reactions in the form of imaginary statements by individuals. This cannot avoid over-simplification and exaggeration but it may serve to bring into the light ideas that might otherwise be indistinct. Of course, no claim is made that any of this represents Quakerism. What perhaps we need is a study to be called 'Towards a Quaker View of Aggression' (as well as one of Love). These views are offered simply as an aid to identifying one's own personal reactions.

First response: 'Why do psychologists always seem to concentrate their attention on the nasty side of life? We all know that violence is bad and that there have been some ugly and dangerous situations. But they are exceptional. They make the headlines and liven-up news bulletins and give us something to think about, if we like that sort of thing. But they are mostly isolated lapses and abnormal. Think of the millions who go through life making the best of it, enjoying the blessings of friends and family, both the young and the old and the rest, content with a modest way of life and grateful to the Creator for what he has given us. We can, in return, help, comfort and cheer our neighbours. Why be made miserable by things at a distance that we can do nothing about? The simple and good things of life are all around us. We should notice them and be thankful. There is no sense in harping-on about football hooligans or vandals. They are a minute minority and publicity only encourages them.'

Second response: 'I have a lot of sympathy with Jung's warnings about collectivism, how it destroys individual responsibility and the appalling results this has on people, especially when they are involved in highly emotional and controversial issues. The Inner Light can be experienced only inwardly, not thrust on us by rabble-rousers or demagogues. We have to reflect on what that Light shows us and, where possible, share this experience with others, quietly and reflectively, not in huge crowds or even small ones. This and the Inner Voice are the source of all true inspiration, all new ideas and thought for others. I think Jung is right to call it each person's own vocation. That has always been the Quaker tradition. Sharing it is wise because one can be misled by some inner drive (no doubt unconscious) that turns out to be egocentric and inappropriate. It seems to me the Quaker structure is designed to guard against collective emotionalism and the risks that follow from it, which Jung mentions. To make the Quaker way work we must try to find a sensitive and continuing balance among us. We see this happening more often in business meetings, though it does arise also in Meeting for Worship. We encounter natural and inevitable differences of view and have to face our own frailties sometimes. But with patience we generally arrive at conclusions or decisions acceptable to all who are present. Jung correctly predicted a rapid increase in collective pressures, in rallies and demonstrations and mass hysteria, all of which are usually aggressive and liable to end in violence. Television and radio surely play a part, too, in this development. They influence our feelings directly, not through reason; unfortunately they generally provoke aggressiveness, not love.

'Generally speaking, Jung's insistence on the unique individual as the only carrier of responsibility for what is right and good, creative and warm-hearted, seems to me timely. So are his warnings about the insidious ways in which State or Party or an organization can reduce us to mere stock units to be counted, classified and used. I think this is in harmony with the spirit of New Testament teaching. Indeed, the events surrounding the martyrdom of Jesus form a vivid archetypal example of primitive irrationality run riot. It first gripped the religious and political authorities and then spread from them to the mob baying for the death of an innocent man. I think we do well to take to heart the psychological meaning of those events. But I do not think propaganda, sermons or demonstrations are any help. I know no better answer than the way Jesus himself showed and taught. Maybe we can help each other to understand its relevance in our very different world today. Such teaching, however, can only gain effect through individuals, not through mass conversions, religious or secular. In fact—through you and me.'

Third response: 'I think this talk about individuals being all that matters is overdone. And I don't accept the much-proclaimed virtues of harmony. Harmony? That sounds fine—which is what harmony is meant to do. But it is not the secret of progress, and never has been. Progress comes through stress and competition and with solidarity, not happy harmony. That may be the dream of the lazy and the incompetent; it is not a secret of success. How can any social change, any improvement in conditions, be brought about except through energetic and like-minded people joining forces, devoted to a common cause? Any change upsets someone and they will try to prevent it. It has to be fought for—not necessarily with violence, but with determination. Union is strength. Together we stand—that sort of thing. Individualism is a polite name for self-indulgence and self-interest. No one can achieve anything worthwhile alone, except perhaps in the arts and even that depends on buyers or audiences. Co-operation is essential to all progress. Vocation is for cranks, drop-outs and a few born leaders. Religion helps us to work together and provides a bond of the 'true followers of Christ'. Therefore we should be willing to evangelize and convert. There is plenty that wants doing. Whether we combine through religion, politics or some other way is not vital, so long as we sink our individuality and work together for a common end.'

Fourth response: 'In my opinion, there is something to be said for each of those views, though one might wish to express oneself a little differently. What I think is most needed is simple clarity. Quakers are not always at their best where clear thinking is needed. Emotion can sometimes be a useful servant but is always a bad master. Jung is certainly right in emphasizing the danger of large groups being carried away by the herd-instinct and collective emotion of any kind, especially aggression. Even mass sentiment leads to nothing constructive and it obscures clear thinking. To express this colloquially, the heart must never be allowed to rule the head. Complex social issues, like complex personal situations, need careful and objective analysis, sometimes with the help or guidance of pro-

163

fessional experts. That is always where we should begin. The necessary action, individual or collective, should follow. Without this reasoned assessment, any collective action is likely to be partisan and provocative and thus intensifies the conflict; in individual difficulties emotional support without such assessment is usually wrong-headed and ineffective, adding fuel to the fires. What is meant to be helpful turns out to be emotional collusion or, in ordinary language, taking sides. That only tends to harden attitudes and increase emotional involvement at the expense (and ultimate extinction) of reason. There is really no substitute for clear thinking, so Jung (I believe) does well by showing what happens when it is neglected: emotion runs amok.'

Perhaps I may be permitted to say that I 'do not necessarily agree with the views expressed' by the imagined characters in this chapter. What is more, agreement or disagreement is not what we are here concerned with, but rather differences in orientation. They are intended to serve as examples of the tension between opposite viewpoints. Somewhat crudely put, they represent two pairs of opposite response, all four of which have a bearing on the tension between vocation and the collective unconscious implicit in the Quaker way: Feeling and thinking (Responses 1 and 4) and introversion and extraversion (Responses 2 and 3).

Vocation (in the sense used by Jung) is a familiar concept to Quakers. We feel drawn, inspired or provoked, all but irresistibly, to a certain course of interest or action in either weighty or trivial affairs. These may be private to us or shared in common with others. Other members help us to assess the appropriateness and value of these urges, to clarify them, and sometimes to restrain us from rash or inexpedient ventures: all this under our shared belief that we strive to live in harmony with supreme values that are greater than our own apprehension of them.

From the collective point of view, there is a crucial difference between bonding together with others to gain power for what we want or, on the contrary, first by ourselves and then with others submitting our urges and callings to the light of the eternal values we jointly acknowledge as pre-eminent. In the first instance, emotion and unrestrained action quickly get out of hand under pressure from the collective unconscious and rash and often violently partisan action follows. What at first seemed a genuine vocational call turns out to be a cloak for personal aggrandisement and an aggressive urge to get our own way. In the second instance our calling is first tested not by our own standard but by transcendent standards.

This has always been the Quaker way. Our concerns are brought to Meeting for Worship or a business meeting, in private discussion or in a small group. This is not merely getting other opinions but asking others to join with us in holding the concern up to the light, seeing it in the light of those values that are eternal. There may well arise a tension of opposite views. This is to be welcomed because, as Jung often pointed out, it is the spark from opposites that provides psychic energy for action in line with our shared values and not simply surging up from the unconscious into violent collective and unconsidered action. This is a subtle but immensely important distinction. The corporate spirituality of a meeting or similar small assembly of worshippers is essential to the experience.

These responses to the tension between personal vocation and the collective unconscious may be illustrated by simple examples that may arise in Quaker meetings. It has been mentioned earlier that Meeting for Worship may be misused as a forum and captive audience to publicize a particular interest or concern and arouse support for it. Or there may be a question of moving to larger premises or building a children's room or using the money in a worthier cause.

Taking part in a local demonstration or carnival may stir conflicting priorities among members. Some may want to mobilize support for a particular local or national or foreign concern, such as the unemployed, AIDS victims, housing, women's rights, starvation, intermediate technology and so forth. We can now see, from our examples, how pressures within a meeting and between individuals may spill over into the spiritual part of the meeting's life and the collective unconscious begins to take precedence. The normal vigilance of elders and overseers and of clerks is the traditional safeguard, but the risk is always present and such interferences may occur at any time.

As already quoted, Jung insisted that spirituality is a treasure that is never superfluous. Since he was writing, the task of integrating the collective unconscious has become more difficult and more urgent and (when achieved) more rewarding. It seems to be the only available safeguard against violent, disruptive and destructive eruptions of primitive unconsciousness.

As we will consider in the next chapter, spirituality has become a life-preserving necessity for mankind rather than a mere treasure. We shall need to consider the relation of transcendence to the collective unconscious that carries its imprint.

13 Symbols of Transcendence

We have been considering the ugly manifestations of the collective unconscious in hatred and aggression that may so quickly burst into crowd violence under the stress of emotion. Not all large crowds are of this kind. Some assemble to celebrate collective joy or sorrow or adulation on great occasions of popular nationalism, others for the fun of singing in a crowd or surrendering to the hypnotic ecstasies of pop music or religious revivalism. Even so, the potential menace inherent in all large gatherings is never far below the surface because of the fatal ease with which mass emotionalism reduces people to a primitive psychic condition. Even highly-regulated and self-disciplined assemblies in theatres, cathedrals or concert halls can erupt into panic or mass disapproval and go berserk if a smell of burning or an affront or explosion activates the collective unconscious.

There is, however, another side to this. The very phrase 'collective unconscious' can be used in two senses. The first is the uncontrolled and primitive emotionalism of a crowd that we have been discussing. The second is the sense in which Jung distinguishes the personal unconscious or shadow from the common, shared unconscious that is part of our inheritance. These are not two separate entities but the same phenomenon seen in its two aspects, the outward and collective and, secondly, the innate and inward psychic equipment of the individual—a kind of unconscious Esperanto of feeling (not of words). If we get caught-up in a crowd the first of these two aspects quickly becomes apparent. We lose our identity and become an undifferentiated and irresponsible unit of the psychic mass.

In opposite conditions, the unconscious operates a different way. If we are alone and quiet, undisturbed and free from urgency, silent and still, out in the countryside or drowsy in the half-light, secure from interruption—then our imagination and phantasy, our wishful thinking, daydreaming, secret anxieties and longings, ambitions and rivalries stir into life in their peculiar undisciplined way, much like dreaming. It is remarkable how seldom such conditions come the way of any of us, at any rate until the second half of life. In the active and preoccupied years we get such interludes rarely unless we are very lucky, perhaps only when we are ill and wakeful, or tired and relaxed.

During the first half of life we are mostly immersed in the reverse of such conditions, bright lights, chatter, interruption, chores, telephone, television, noise of traffic and aeroplanes. These go on almost incessantly for very many of us so that we become dependent on them, slightly scared of solitude, half-light and silence, or in desperation cultivate some artificial technique of contemplation or meditation to get a bit of peace and quiet. All too easily a vicious circle builds up around us in which we rob ourselves of the sustenance our life could derive from this neglected source.

'Seek to know an inward retirement even amid the activities of daily life', say the Advices. 'Make a quiet place wherein you may learn more of the meaning of prayer'.[1] How wise and necessary, but how difficult, how unconventional in the way we live now. Send the children out, turn off the television, take the phone off the hook, put Do Not Disturb on the door, insert the ear plugs, invent a headache (if all else fails). And then it will be your own conscience that disturbs you. 'Don't forget this, you ought to do that, how are you going to manage the other?' For most of us there is not much chance of sustained quiet except at Sunday Meeting. No wonder we prize it so highly, with its ordered calm and corporate stillness. 'Come with heart and mind prepared'[2] we are counselled. But we must be lucky and skilful and resolute to achieve such preparation. No wonder we may forget (or even find it hard to believe) that the collective unconscious has a personal and private aspect which may be a source of unrivalled originality, inspiration, joy and good ideas. The necessary conditions for its activity were well understood by our Quaker forbears and it is a precious tradition they have passed on to us. Such opportunities are otherwise so rare today that it is no wonder the sinister and destructive aspect of the collective unconscious so often runs rife.

Experience of Meeting for Worship suggests that the inner voice maintains some kind of dialogue between our normal, conscious, moral self and the personal unconscious, as it were interpreting the one to the other. But in the end it is the conscious self that speaks in ministry. Quakers are familiar with the interior tension on such occasions and this is entirely in harmony with Jung's observations about the spark of opposites that yields something new and constructive. This is how the uniqueness of the individual self is fostered and Jung viewed it as of the greatest significance in resisting pressure from 'the blind laws of nature that move the masses'.[3] He asked 'Who can hope to withstand the overwhelming force that is drawing people like a maelstrom?'[4] Only those, he maintained, who are rooted in both the inner and the outer world.

This has, I suggest, always been a Quaker belief. It is a lonely task and means facing one's own uniqueness, taking responsibility for one's own attempt to grow towards psychic integration. He called being alone with one's own self 'the most decisive experience of all'.[5] Referring to psychotherapy, he wrote 'The patient must be alone if he is to find out what it is that supports him when he can no longer support himself,'[6]—surely a thought that might have been expressed in almost identical terms by a spiritual director.

Jung saw the relevance of Christian symbolism to this same fundamental basis of personality. 'This apparently unique life (he wrote) became a sacred symbol because it is the psychological prototype of the only meaningful life.'[7] He saw the deification of Jesus and (in some sects) of the Buddha also, as evidence of the supreme value of an ideal of personality that follows its own inner law. It is both a psychological and a religious truth that, as Jung put it, 'man's life should be sacrificial, that is, offered up to an idea greater than himself'.[8] The task is to find one's own conviction and that cannot be achieved without finding a degree of harmony between inner and outer, conscious and unconscious, individual and collective. We now must look at the path that leads in that direction.

According to Jung, 'the harmonizing of conscious and unconscious data . . . is an irrational life-process which expresses itself in definite symbols'.[9] New attitudes and situations emerge. He called this process the 'transcendent function'. It is a union or harmony of opposites. The supreme importance of this lifelong task has been voiced by philosophers, mystics and masters of Eastern religion and philosophy down the ages. For us the significance of Jung's contribution to the task is his indication of what is concerned in it and how it may be approached. In his last, autobiographical book he explained his view that the great Christian myth must accept monotheism (the doctrine of a '"dark antagonist" alongside the omnipotent God')[10] and reject dualism. He commented 'Only thus can the One God be granted the wholeness and the synthesis of opposites which should be His' and called the incarnation 'the essence of the Christian message'.[11]

A little earlier in the same passage he gave a hint as to how this fundamental task may be approached: 'Symbols, by their very nature, can so unite the opposites that these no longer diverge or clash, but mutually supplement one another'.[12] They give meaning to life. It is therefore to myths and symbols, not to reason or feeling, that we must look in order to develop the transcendent function. The symbols that he is referring to emerge spontaneously from the unconscious and are absorbed into consciousness, a process that seems to be endemic to human nature from the earliest times and characteristic of both primitive and civilized people.

It is necessary here to contrast Jung's reference to symbols with the popular understanding of the Freudian use of the same term. In Freudian terms symbols are normally equated with a conscious equivalent, often (though not exclusively) sexual in character, almost as though they are terms of a foreign language which the user speaks but does not understand, but which the analyst is trained to understand and, when appropriate, to interpret so that the patient is helped to realize what he was unconsciously trying to convey. From Jung's point of view this is almost a mechanistic procedure. To his way of thinking, symbols emerge spontaneously from the collective unconscious, as it were autonomously and in their own right. Even a Jungian analyst cannot say with assurance what each 'means' as it emerges. He has to observe the way it merges into the conscious thought and feeling of the patient, as it were to let it have its say, remembering that symbols are universal to mankind and innate, though each individual reacts to them, relates to them and uses them in his (or her) own unique way.

Here we are concerned with therapeutic ideas only so far as they throw light on the religious (particularly the Quaker) way to personal wholeness as the task facing each one of us. It is opportune, therefore, to consider just what kind of myths and symbols are relevant to this task and how their presence may best be used.

We can learn to recognize the 'language' of symbolism through dreams and when we are relaxed (as outlined earlier in this chapter) in reverie and day dreaming. We encounter myths outside ourselves, in stories, opera, ballet, poetry, pictures, sculpture, reading. Sometimes they pass us by, at other times they unaccountably grip and fascinate us when they speak to our unconscious condition. This sometimes happens in Meeting for Worship. It is distinct from the more usual experience in which one is aware of a gain in insight into some aspect of one's personal life, a new way of seeing an old difficulty, as happens regularly during counselling or psychotherapy. Parts of the shadow become conscious and therefore open to our own critical judgment and we become less prone to projection.

The impact on us of symbols and archetypes from the collective unconscious is a transcendent experience, deeper and more impressive than this. It is what makes some meetings peculiarly significant and what many Quakers value most highly. When the collective unconscious is stirred, an individual is deeply affected. It is an encounter with that which is holy, numinous, transcendent—a spiritual experience. An imaginary example will serve to illustrate this critical distinction.

A regular, middle-sized, Sunday morning Meeting for Worship assembles, with flickers of greeting and recognition as the members and any visitors settle down. After a short while the children leave and the silence gathers. No one speaks. A remote dog barks. An aeroplane passes overhead. Somewhere a child is laughing. Sparrows chirp and flutter in the clematis outside. Half an hour or so goes by.

Furtively, a member glances down at a Bible and opens it. She hesitates. During the past week she heard a fine performance of Haydn's oratorio *The Creation*. The long, strange, almost timeless introduction made a special impression on her. She remembers thinking of the passage as 'the music of silence'. Then she became absorbed in both the libretto and the glorious music and the unfolding story. She had been amused by some of the wording, presumably translated into German and back again into English. When she was home again she had looked up the Authorised Version, with the sense of Haydn's music at the back of her mind.

Now, in Meeting, she felt urged to speak of it and is alarmed to find she is on her feet. She has a good ear and reads well, slowly and clearly.

> 'In the beginning God created the heaven and the earth. And the earth was without form, and void, and darkness was upon the face of the deep. And the Spirit of God moved upon the face of the waters. And God said, Let there be light: and there was light. And God saw the light, that it was good.'[13]

As she comes to the words 'and there was light', that tremendous burst of music returns to her mind and her voice quivers a little with excitement. It had been like the sudden initial burst of fireworks at some royal celebration, rocketing up into the blue-black sky and bursting into golden light. She pauses, not quite sure how to go on. Then she describes with relish the performance she had heard and the joy it gave her. She sits down. An elder glances at his watch. The stillness seems stiller than ever. 'Elizabeth reads well' someone thinks inwardly, 'I think she had drama lessons. She has a good voice'. 'Odd, (thinks another), how dramatic that old legend still is and how easily one takes it for granted. It's a wonderful opening for the Bible.' 'How enviable (thinks a third person) to believe it was all as simple as that. What gave God the idea, I wonder. Was he bored, out there in dark chaos? What a pity we can't still believe it literally. Science has spoilt it—intelligence—the Garden of Eden—disobedience—hubris—the bomb—nemesis—the Greeks were not fools—where *was* I?'.

And over there, as still and quiet as the rest, sits another member, startled and excited, smiling but not knowing why, his pulse thudding in his ears. What has struck him? He doesn't know. He has nothing to say. He is too confused to think straight. Anyway, what is there to say? Light—that's what we all crave. He recalls the King of Denmark: '"Give me some light: away!" All: "Lights, lights, lights"'.[14] Chaos, darkness, doubts, ignorance—and then God said 'Let there be light: *and there was light'*.[15] Now he is on his feet, with nothing to say. 'Light? (he says, uncertainly) Light. Isn't that what we all crave for? (He quotes the prayer from his childhood). "Lighten our darkness, we beseech thee, O Lord"'. He sits down, rather bemused, wondering what the meeting will make of it. 'I wonder what's stirred old George' thinks someone, 'Something has'.

There is more ministry on the topic of light and enlightenment, inner light, darkness and being benighted, the star in the East. Someone quotes 'I am come a light into the world'.[16] Some of this is predictable, some of it fresh and original, some of it tense and tentative, some confident and reassuring. 'Rather too much ministry, I thought,' someone says on the way out afterwards.

Now another imaginary meeting, the following week. Before the children have left someone begins: 'I daresay you find (as I do) that some simple little stories stick in your mind. One of *my* favourites is about Jesus. It doesn't come from the Bible but it has often been told about him. Well, one day he was walking with some of his friends along a hot, dusty road. Presently they came to a group of children crowded round something lying at the side of the road. They were making little cries of disgust. You know the sort of thing: 'Ugh! How horrible. Look at the flies. Pooh, what a pong'. It was a dead mangy cat lying there in the dust, its mouth open. Not a very nice thing to come across, was it? Jesus came up to see. He smiled and said to the children 'Just look what beautiful teeth he had'.

This was followed by a short moral, about noticing the good and nice things in life, not just the nasty and ugly ones—seeing the best in people, not put off by something we don't like about them. It ended with a reference to 'answering that of God in everyone'.[17] (George Fox).

After the children had left the same theme was developed in ministry, seeing the best in people, not judging by first impressions, looking always for the good, the true and the beautiful.

Anyone familiar with Quaker Meetings will, I think, have encountered these two different kinds of Meeting. Some of us prefer the one approach, some the other. Some are helped by the one rather than the other. Some are at home with the one but at sea with the other. In this present context there is a critical distinction to be made. In the second example (addressed to the children) there was no spark of opposites. It was a clear and simple piece of religious instruction, thought-out beforehand. It was ministry at a conscious, moral, two-dimensional level, though with implications that anyone could apply to their own self ('Why do I flinch from people with loud voices?').

The tone is relaxed, conversational, perhaps just a little patronizing. The moral is simple and direct. Jesus gives to the moral a benediction, a certainty that this is what we, too, should do. There are no overtones of mystery or spirituality, no symbolical truth or new way to see an old experience. There are clear-cut alternatives, one good, one bad. There is nothing inward-looking, nothing uncertain, nothing controversial, nothing to disturb the complacency of believing we can do whatever we are enjoined to do so long as it has a religious base.

That little story was flat and rather contrived, a mini-sermon. It had a moral but no inspiration. The ministry that followed seems to have been at the same level, as often happens. In all, it was a complete contrast to the previous meeting and its ministry. The first contribution, the reading from Genesis and the account of the music, was voiced tentatively, not a set piece. The link between the oratorio and the Genesis myth had stirred something in the first speaker. She did not know what, why or how. She brought the bible with her and wondered whether to read the passage or not. So half-an-hour passed in silence. But she was urged inwardly to describe her experience, to bring it out into the Meeting and see what followed.

As she recaptured the experience there was tension in her voice, especially at the climax 'and there was light.' Her words found no resonance in the first few people mentioned in the account of the Meeting, only simple thoughts unstirred by inward feeling. But in George, in the corner, her words and the feeling behind them sparked-off a response and spoke to his condition. Evidently this was something to do with light and darkness symbolizing insight and ignorance or conscious and unconscious. For him, it was an experience of what Jung calls the transcendent function. The symbolism of chaos and creator, light and darkness, alerted him inwardly. No doubt he will continue to think about it and work out what it means for him. These are symbols from the collective unconscious and they often, like many others, play a vivid and continuing part in our development.

Something stirred also among those who followed the ministry and his contribution to it. They filled-out the scope of the symbols in ways that came to mind naturally, in this way helping not only the first two who ministered but anyone present who was at that time susceptible to the same challenge.

Jung makes some suggestions for fostering this process

that comes so readily in Meeting for Worship. We can open ourselves to some extent to be sensitive to symbols of transcendence, if we know how. We cannot force their presence but we can learn to be receptive, not only on Sundays but all the time. 'Constant observation (wrote Jung) pays the unconscious a tribute that more or less guarantees its co-operation'.[18]

Our imagination can be allowed free play, once we have learnt to trust it. It will emerge spontaneously, in its own time and own way, often surprisingly, through archetypes and symbols. Many of them are familiar to all of us as part of the inner mythology we all share—fire, wind, sea, a mother-figure, the young hero, sun and moon, the wise old man, certain animals both real and mythological, like dragons and unicorns. Shapes and sounds affect us unaccountably sometimes, movement as in ballet or ice-skating, clouds, birds, fairy stories, opera—all the vast world of the imagination opens to us once we learn to value it and heed what comes from it. All this opens-up a landscape of transcendent symbolism, of archetypes and dreams, of art and nature, that enfolds us and to which our Western way of life so often blinds us. Underlying it all and all the opposites is 'God as the guiding principle of unity within the depths of the psyche',[19] that Anthony Storr spoke of.

We are not wise to try to pin-down experience of transcendence in definitions or analyse it into words. We shall know it from the excitement it brings to us, the sense of mystery and awe as well as joy. Not everyone can respond to the idealism of Romantic poetry, but to those who do, Shelley's lyrical drama *Prometheus Unbound* is an outstanding source of archetypal images and symbolism, too abstract for some readers but strangely inspiring for others. There is a well-known but mysterious passage, near the beginning, that T. S. Eliot uses in his play *The Cocktail Party* (itself deeply symbolical of many of the themes raised by Jung and quoted in this book). The Earth addresses Prometheus:

Ere Babylon was dust,
The Magus Zoroaster, my dead child,
Met his own image walking in the garden.
That apparition, sole of men, he saw.
For know there are two worlds of life and death:
One that which thou beholdest; but the other
Is underneath the grave, where do inhabit
The shadows of all forms that think and live
Till death unite them and they part no more;
Dreams and the light imaginings of men,
And all that faith creates or love desires,
Terrible, strange, sublime and beauteous shapes.[20]

(For anyone not familiar with this kind of poetry, it might be added that for the Romantics death was often used not literally but as a symbol of union with the divine, with the beloved or with nature).

Such symbols of transcendence and unity are not for all of us and it should not be thought Jung implied that transcendence is only for those who are introverted or artistic in their psychic orientation. As mentioned earlier in this book, there are many whose way lies not through receptiveness but through activity, sometimes in unpretentious crafts or pastimes or even chores: these give them the same access to the mysterious realm of transcendence recognized by Jung as vocation.

The distinction is not in the activity or interest but in the meaning it has, an indefinable but vivid sense of rightness or 'rightness for me', compounded of joy and a particular kind of loving acceptance and dedication. For those receptive to it, transcendence gives life a meaning, no matter what symbols it uses. Walter de la Mare expressed this point in a warning, in words that might surely have been Blake's:

Loving delight forgot,
Life's very roots must rot.[21]

As for Jung, he ended a short book published only three

years before his death with the assertion that, if we truly understand the Christian message, we shall realize it is within each individual that 'even God seeks his goal'.[22]

14 A Reasonable Faith

In this final chapter we shall consider how far and in what ways Jung's ideas (outlined in these pages) may speak to our condition.

This famous Quaker phrase implies that something has alerted our attention, has some relevance for us and challenges us in ways that we had not entirely foreseen. In spite of a basic unity of faith and practice and a corporate sense of enduring values, not all Quakers think alike or see life in quite the same way. Our 'condition' is thus special to each one, even though we share many of the same concerns. When something speaks to our condition we have to answer in our own terms, not as any hierarchy requires of us.

Jung's ideas and discoveries arose out of his analytical experience with the hundreds of patients who consulted him, as well as from research and study. Much of what he wrote is in harmony with the Quaker way, for instance his belief that religion should be founded on experience, at first hand rather than on dogma or doctrine; that no one can tolerate a life devoid of meaning; that the spiritual part of us is as real as the physical, the emotional and the intellectual; that our inner life is as important as our outer experience; that a working harmony of differences and opposites is a mature achievement and a sign of psychological health; that an inner voice prompts us and an inner light guides us towards our personal vocation; that God is present in all human nature as well as transcendent; that faith and practice are two expressions of the same reality— our human responsibility.

Here is surely enough to give us heart to face what else he shows us, not of course in order to follow it blindly, but to give it a measure of our discernment. What he offers a reader is insight (apt word!) into human nature and the human predicament, a deeper understanding of our fellow beings and of our own personality and of the terms on which our lives are lived: new light, provided we can see by it.

Psychology may be used to provide a detached and objective interpretation of the way people think and feel but when our condition is spoken to we are stirred inwardly and sometimes with painful surprise or inner excitement. The possibility of discomfort cannot be evaded. Evelyn Underhill wrote in her classic work on mysticism of the price one must expect to pay for spiritual progress: 'That law of the inner life, which sounds so fantastic and yet is so bitterly true—"No progress without pain"—asserts itself. It declares that birth pangs must be endured in the spiritual as well as in the material world'.[1] Seventeen years later, Jung wrote much the same thing in an article on 'Marriage as a Psychological Relationship': 'There is no coming to consciousness without pain'.[2] It can hardly be otherwise, since what lies in the personal unconscious has been defensively repressed and it takes courage to face it.

Readers, hearers or worshippers, we are all of us in some respects like the inhabitants of Plato's famous mythical cave.[3] They had been chained all their lives so that they could see only shadows on the wall, thrown by objects and people outside the entrance. They inevitably took these shadows for reality, for they had never seen anything else. When at last they were released and saw real objects in the light outside, they were dazzled and bewildered.

When Jung wrote of the need to teach people the art of seeing and to listen to their own nature, he was referring to the development of insight and self-awareness, so vitally necessary in an environment heavily biased towards extraversion as our Western way of life is. He knew that this would be a thankless and difficult task. He acknowledged that no one wanted to hear the things he had to tell them. But every gain in insight is a step towards personal wholeness, however humiliating or uncomfortable it may be when someone speaks to our condition.

It is now our task to ask what aspects of Jung's writings may speak to us in this way. He did not share the healthy-minded conviction that God is all-wise, all-loving and all-powerful, with no dark side. He was convinced of mono-theism, that God embraces all there is and is the ultimate union of all opposites. This contrasts with the dualistic conviction of Zoroaster and with the polytheistic pantheon of Hinduism or the classical assembly of gods and god-desses under the supreme authority of Zeus (or Jupiter). It contrasts also with the more recent conventional and pop-ular view of Christianity that God is all good and Satan the embodiment of evil and both of them at perpetual warfare in the human heart. Jung did not confuse God with the unconscious. He believed that God communicates with us through the collective unconscious and the imagina-tion, through the mysterious grace of creativity and inspiration, through the voice of our inner calling or voca-tion and through the evil, mystery and terror and suffering that lurk in the inner darkness, in our surroundings and our personal fate.

In Jung's view an inability to accept the dual nature of God makes it all-too-easy to claim that the best of the inner voice is the voice of God and to disown the inner urge to evil as the temptation of the Devil. Jung, I believe, would have understood and sympathised with the peasant woman in Emile Zola's novel *The Earth*: when a sudden storm ruined the year's crop on which her family liveli-hood depended, she flung stones furiously at the sky and screamed: 'You dirty pig up there! Why can't you leave us alone?'.[4]

Jung insisted that the unconscious is neither all-good nor all-evil but morally neutral and that it is the respon-sibility of our conscious judgment to make moral distinc-tions and choices. Many people still suspect that the unconscious is something evil and sinister or at best sub-versive of our consciously good intentions and ideals. They cannot accept the moral neutrality of the collective unconscious nor the compensatory nature of the personal shadow. It is reassuring to see goodness as that of God immanent within (and a part of our nature) and evil as distinct, outside, transcendent. Jung showed that this view enables one to project evil onto others, seeing it wholly or chiefly in enemies, criminals, rivals—anywhere except within. This is no way towards wholeness and psychic health, nor to tolerance and love. It contradicts Christ's injunction to love our enemies and prevents our recognizing that of evil in our own hearts. Jung supported the wholesome doctrine of original sin, so unpopular today.

Jung's view of the unconscious shadow as an essential counterpart to the ego (or conscious part of the psyche) is similarly unacceptable to many people, even though no one can ignore our occasional Freudian slips on the banana-skin of the unconscious. So we laugh to make light of the embarrassment they cause us, for they speak all too eloquently to our condition.

He was equally convinced of the significance of myth and symbol and legend incorporating universal concepts expressed in art and religion, ritual and superstition. Hence he developed his concept of the collective unconscious and today only the most practical, extraverted and literal-minded rationalists can deny the formidable influence that this mysterious realm may have upon us, the inspiration of true art, experience of the numinous and of the ideal world of the spirit, the nightmare terror of the haunting dream-world of Frankenstein's monster, of the Divine Comedy or the Ancient Mariner, the Heaven and Hell of William Blake, the paintings of Hieronymus Bosch, the chaotic struggle and ultimate triumph of the Choral Symphony, the heart-rending power of the Saint Matthew Passion or the formidable illustrations of Gustav Doré: all this is as much a part of our world as space-travel or a supermarket.

Jung suggested that our modern over-emphasis on the outer world and under-valuing of the inner world is a dangerous distortion. He proclaimed the value of phantasy as an essential factor in psychic wholeness and believed that the way we live now is spiritually starved and out of balance, leaving us in the grip of the dark and threatening and destructive side of the collective unconscious.

For some Christians, perhaps the most provocative of Jung's conceptions is that opposites may be complementary and both of them valid, that the spark of contrast between them may be a source of inspiration and creativity, of harmony (not unison) and originality. We are so fatally used to treating opposites as alternatives, one of which must be fought and if possible destroyed. Acceptance does not mean agreement or condonation. It is the way towards wholeness, integration, and to co-operation rather than enmity, reasonableness rather than fanatical extremism, goodwill instead of hatred. Acceptance is an act of faith but it is reasonable faith, opening the way for balance between extremes, moderate and amenable to reason. It is the marriage of opposites from which springs a new birth. War between antagonists is sterile.

The practical application of this faith will perhaps make the issue clearer than do these abstractions. For an example we may return to psychotherapy. As described earlier, people usually consult a therapist or counsellor because some crisis has arisen which they cannot resolve. They may know what they should do but are unable to do it. The preliminary focus of discussion is dual—what the crisis is and what it represents in emotional terms to the one who is troubled by it. Only free discussion, prompted by a friendly and non-partisan listener will help to bring out the relevant facts and the inner feelings arising from their impact on the client or patient.

When emotions are accepted without criticism a new level of intimate and free discussion becomes possible. The persona is laid aside with relief and inner feelings begin to be exposed without disguise—the good and the bad, the loving and the destructive, ambitions and anxieties, anger, fear, sorrow, belief and doubt, hope and despair. The therapist seeks only to help the other person to 'bring the invisible into the light'.[5] The chaos of confused and opposite feelings becomes more manageable.

This brief summary, necessarily over-simplified, may perhaps only make sense to someone who has experienced the relief and growth of insight from turning to a friend or counsellor with enough empathy and insight and interested concern to refrain from criticism, expressed or implied or even felt. There are people with a natural gift for this healing role. Adequate training widens its scope and deepens their insight. A prerequisite in the would-be helper is to be unafraid of strong and opposite feelings, values, prejudices and convictions. Such a discussion is, in Quaker terms, a joint and co-operative confrontation with the 'condition' of the one who is distressed.

The task of the helper is to offer, without strings of any kind, the experience of being accepted no matter what is brought into the sharing. In Jung's terms, the acceptance of opposites is what makes possible a constructive outcome and a way to cope with a difficulty that was insurmountable. The steady growth of available counselling services of different varieties is a beneficent alternative to moral injunction or practical advice (which only helps those who are able to act on it), though the need is still much greater than the facilities.

It may be helpful here, as an illustration, to describe a simple experiment based on these same principles. It was not intended as a substitute for personal counselling nor was it based on any particular difficulty or distress. It was, though, founded on the principles of training counsellors and to illustrate the practical value of accepting opposites.

The project was offered, in a Quaker context, under the general heading of 'What canst *thou* say?' and consisted of a series of meetings that would be something between free discussion and Meeting for Worship. The object was to give members of the group an opportunity to voice their own beliefs and experience and then hear others discuss them. The way of working was as follows.

There were six weekly meetings and those who joined were asked to be sure of attending each one, though of course anyone was free to drop out (but not return). There was a limit of ten members and each meeting lasted an hour and a half. Each started with silence for about fifteen minutes. Then one of the group spoke for not more than fifteen minutes along the general line of 'What I believe and why'. This speaker then remained a listener until the final stage about an hour later, while the rest of the members discussed what had been said.

If direct questions were put to the one who had spoken first, the convener interrupted to remind members that the introducer was to remain silent until after the others had finished discussing. In this way the focus was kept on what the introducer had said and what each member made of it. This might include agreement or disagreement, a doubt about what was meant, a wish for more detail or a description of comparable experiences or beliefs or doubts.

Some fifteen minutes before the end of the meeting, the convener invited the introducer to comment on the discussion. There was then a brief silence and the meeting closed.

The six introducers had volunteered, with a little encouragement, the first one being one of the elders of the Meeting. The convener took no part in the discussion unless it got bogged down or dried up. The same convener was present at each meeting and kept as inconspicuous as possible.

It is important that the convener should not intrude his or her own views or offer any kind of criticism of what has been said, or take any active part except perhaps to help things along if they get stuck or gently restrain too much digression (for the sake of the introducer). After these meetings had ended, the group met informally to evaluate the experiment and consider how it could be improved. However, no changes were thought to be necessary.

A few further comments are relevant. Membership of these groups included members and attenders, most of them fairly new. The method encourages participants to speak openly and frankly but avoids argument. The unofficial and experimental character of the venture minimises any tendency to say what is perhaps expected and helps members to voice their own ideas however controversial or tentative. A most impressive spirit of openness and friendly commitment, at once serious and light-hearted and sometimes tense, developed among both groups. They used to remain behind, talking among themselves, after the meeting had ended and the convener had departed. This spontaneous informality was perhaps as fruitful as the rest of the evening, though it could not have happened without it.

Most members valued particularly the unusual experience of hearing their views and beliefs discussed by others without themselves taking part and either defending or explaining themselves. They had a chance, of course, to explain any misunderstanding when released from their role of listener in the final stage. Throughout the two series there were plenty of contrasting beliefs and experiences and different priorities of value.

This type of meeting seems to suit particularly those who are seekers rather than faithful followers and are concerned but not rigidly committed. Any eagerness to suggest what others ought to believe should be restrained by the convener if it should inadvertently arise. A weighty Friend, eager to propound Quakerism in the cause of evangelistic 'outreach' would have been out of place, however helpful for a meeting set-up for that purpose.

The structure of these meetings was designed to provide a secure and easy atmosphere without the pressure of question and answer. It is much more personal than Meeting for Worship and tends to be more varied. The convener's role is crucial. He or she should take a mainly background role but be ready to begin and end the meeting, deal with any practical rearrangements and be vigilant to discourage unhelpful altercation or rivalry but tolerant of any views sincerely held, whether or not they are consistent with the Quaker way. On the whole, this experiment gave good effect to the Advice 'Seek to know one another in the things which are eternal'.[6] It could no doubt be adapted for use with other topics, though the way of working should be explained in detail to those who will be taking part.

'The living spirit grows and even outgrows its earlier forms of expression (wrote Jung), . . . Measured against it, the names and forms which men have given it mean little enough'.[7]

It is fair, I think, at this stage to imagine a reader objecting that this chapter may be reasonable, but it is not a faith. The acceptance of opposites and speaking to someone's condition are equally relevant in humanist or agnostic circles and do not depend on faith. 'Helping people by means of counselling (an objector might say) is an extension of non-directive social casework and an application of the principles of psychotherapy. It is not a religious activity. Of course, some counsellors and psychotherapists (like some of their clients) are religious people and have an active faith. But it is equally true that many have not. Being of service to others, or turning to others oneself when in a fix, are not special to religion or to religious people nor are they expressions of a religious faith. Where, then, does this living spirit come in? Is it another name for God or is it something independent of religion?'

Some Quakers raise similar objections when they feel that special interest groups (such as Universalists or the Inter-Faith group) have abandoned the fundamental Christian faith of the original Quakers. Jung's point is nevertheless valid: the living spirit is more important than the name or form in which it is proclaimed and served. It cannot reasonably be confined to those who are affiliated to any one religion or sect. It may be found in any religion. This same objection is sometimes held against seekers by the faithful followers. Perhaps such differences are but growing-pains or birth-pangs of the living spirit along the Quaker way. So long as there are sparks of difference between them, something fresh and constructive is possible. If either takes over and excludes the other, we are stuck in fundamentalism.

The long tradition of God's masculinity and absolute power and authority is, for many thoughtful and sensitive people, no longer supportable. Doctrinal and specialist interpretations of scripture (not to mention the Thirty-nine Articles of Faith or contemporary pronouncements by scholars and Church authorities) no longer speak to the condition of many Christians. Religious experience, however, is undeniably real for many people. Whether they speak of the inner light or the living spirit or the presence of God is semantic rather than vital. None of these and similar names denies the experience of transcendence or the power of myth and symbol or the reality of the numinous and the awesome effect of its presence.

In Shelley's elegy for Keats he wrote:

The One remains, the many change and pass;
Heaven's light forever shines, Earth's shadows fly;
Life, like a dome of many-coloured glass,
Stains the white radiance of Eternity.[8]

The various forms that have been (and are) given to religious experience need not obscure its reality. Like poets, we have all to find whatever best expresses the reality, knowing that it cannot adequately portray the eternal radiance.

A practical application of this view is that we should welcome the clash and sparkle of opposites, provided it is not mere altercation or competitive argument. Meeting for Worship provides a natural source of spiritual experience when it speaks to our condition. The kind of discussion described in this chapter serves the same end for those who can make use of it. Both ways are open to spiritual reality as, for others, are the more highly-structured religious services (especially the Eucharist) or the rigorous practice of meditation, retreats, or Zen training. Others gain experience of the living spirit through nature or works of art when approached (as Quakers are advised to approach Meeting for Worship) 'with heart and mind prepared',[9] that is to say in a relaxed, receptive, tranquil and expectant frame of mind. Silence and solitude (shared or alone) are both necessary, an opening of the self and a stillness of attention.

All this is characteristic of Quaker worship. It is not subservient or routine or a perfunctory expression of thanks or praise, but more like awaiting the arrival of somebody loved and revered. 'The real work of prayer is done by God, (wrote an American, Elizabeth Hunter, for an anthology)—our part is to empty the heart of those things which keep Him out'.[10]

For those who see God best in terms of personality, this aptly describes the Quaker attitude to worship and the necessary preparation for it. Others may prefer a different way of expressing the same truth. The Quaker way of worship means union with the living spirit (or with God), however transitory, a spark of contact between opposites, a union from which new life may spring.

In the religious life, as in the mental and emotional, the compulsion to see opposites as alternatives and not as complementary is the principal bar to harmony, maturity, wholeness and growth of the psyche. Only an attitude of acceptance can remove this obstacle. Therapy can help us in our emotional and mental life: in the life of the spirit we have to find ways of worship that speak to our individual spiritual condition. Acceptance is a cold, formal term for love, that degraded word. Many years ago I heard a stipendiary magistrate describe something that happened in his juvenile court. After hearing a long list of misdemeanours, he asked the mother of the boy before him what she had to say. She replied at once 'He is a good boy, your worship, bar what he does'.

Psychotherapy provides the experience of acceptance bar what one does, and is similarly unconditional. It becomes a faith only if it includes the spark and ultimate union of opposites in the divine principle of harmony. For some, this is celebrated in the triumphant assertion that God is love. For the nature-loving Wordsworth—

> the immortal spirit grows
> Like harmony in music; there is a dark
> Inscrutable workmanship that reconciles
> Discordant elements, makes them cling together
> In one society.[11]

A reasonable faith can be built around either of these two convictions and be consistent with Jung's teaching and the Quaker way. But—

> Only love can redeem
> This truth, that delight;
> Bring morning to blossom again
> Out of plague-ridden night;
> Restore to the lost the found,
> To the blinded, sight.[12]

References

CHAPTER 1

[1] *Jung: Selected Writings.* Selected and Introduced by Anthony Storr. London: Fontana, 1983, p. 262.
[2] Jung (C. G.) *Psychology and Alchemy* (Collected Works Vol. 12). London: Routledge & Kegan Paul, 2nd edn., 1953, para. 14.
[3] *Matthew,* 5:14 (AV).
[4] *I John,* 1:5 (AV).
[5] *I Corinthians,* 13:12 (AV).
[6] *Psychological Reflections: an anthology of the writings of C. G. Jung.* Selected and edited by Jolande Jacobi from the first German edition 1945. New York: Pantheon Books Inc., Bollinger Series, Vol. 13, p. 316 or London: Routledge & Kegan Paul (Ark Paperbacks), 1986, p. 351 (N.B. In this new edition the material has been revised by the Editor and some of the translation modified, some new extracts are included and some earlier ones omitted).
[7] Jung (C. G.) *Modern Man in Search of a Soul.* Trans. by W. S. Dell and Cary T. Baynes. London: Routledge & Kegan Paul, 1933.
[8] *Jung: Selected Writings,* op. cit., p. 261.
[9] Ibid., p. 403.
[10] Ibid., p. 355.
[11] *Psychological Reflections,* op. cit., p. 144, or Ark edn., p. 162.
[12] Ibid., p. 137, or Ark edn., p. 155.
[13] *Jung: Selected Writings,* op. cit., p. 385.
[14] Ibid., p. 375.
[15] Ibid., p. 393.
[16] Ibid., p. 375.
[17] Ibid., p. 376.
[18] Alexander (M.) *Hymns Ancient and Modern,* No. 573.
[19] *Jung: Selected Writings,* op. cit., p. 26.
[20] *Christian Faith and Practice in the Experience of the Society of Friends (CFP).* London Yearly Meeting, 1960, rptd. with minor corrections 1961 and 1963. This is the first volume of the 'Book of Christian Discipline', the principal Quaker book of British Friends. The second volume is *Church Government.* London Yearly Meeting, 1968, rev. rpt. 1980.
[21] James (William) *The Varieties of Religious Experience* (Gifford Lectures 1901–2). London: Collins, Fontana paperbacks, 9th impression, 1979, lectures IV & V.
[22] *Jung: Selected Writings,* op. cit., p. 321.
[23] *John,* 10:30 (AV).
[24] *Jung: Selected Writings,* op. cit., p. 258.

CHAPTER 2

[1] *Modern Man in Search of a Soul,* op. cit., p. 273.
[2] *Jung: Selected Writings,* op. cit., p. 249.
[3] Ibid., p. 353.
[4] *Pschological Reflections,* op. cit., p. 300, or Ark edn., p. 338.

5 Ibid., p. 179 or Ark edn., p. 199–200.
6 Ibid., p. 268 or Ark edn. p. 301.
7 Jung (C. G.) *The Development of Personality* (Collected Works Vol. 17). London: Routledge & Kegan Paul, 1954.
8 Gorman (George H.) *The Amazing Fact of Quaker Worship* (1973 Swarthmore Lecture). London: Quaker Home Service, 1973, rptd. 1979 & 1988.
9 *Jung: Selected Writings*, op. cit., p. 257.
10 Ibid., p. 25.
11 *Psychological Reflections*, op. cit., p. 317, or Ark edn., p. 353.
12 *Jung: Selected Writings*, op. cit., p. 87.
13 Ibid., p. 90.
14 Ibid., p. 88.
15 Ibid., p. 243.
16 Ibid., p. 281.
17 George Fox, *Journal*, ed. by John L. Nickalls. London Yearly Meeting, 1952, rptd. 1975, p. 263. Quoted in *CFP*, op. cit. §376.
18 *Psychological Reflections*, op. cit., p. 198 or Ark edn., p. 222.
19 Ibid., p. 197 or Ark edn., p. 221.
20 Ibid., p. 192 or Ark edn., p. 214.
21 Ibid., p. 143 or Ark edn., p. 161.

CHAPTER 3
1 Jung (C. G.) *Memories, Dreams, Reflections*. London: Collins and Kegan Paul, 1963, also Fount Paperbacks (Flamingo edn). 1983, p. 249.
2 *Jung: Selected Writings*, op. cit., p. 91.
3 Horney (Karen) *Self Analysis*. London: Routledge & Kegan Paul, 1957.
4 *Psychological Reflections*, op. cit., p. 287 or Ark edn., p. 322.
5 Soren Kierkegaard quoted in *Texts and Pretexts* by Aldous Huxley. London: Chatto & Windus.
6 *Development of Personality*, op. cit., p. 195.
7 Ibid., p. 175.
8 Ibid., p. 194.
9 Ibid., p. 192.
10 Macmurray (John) 'What is Religion?' in *The Listener*, 13 December 1956.
11 *Matthew*, 5:28 (AV).
12 *John*, 8:3, 4. (AV).
13 *Development of Personality*, op. cit., p. 94.
14 *Church Government*, op. cit., §702 'Advices & Queries' III.
15 Bettelheim (Bruno) *The Informed Heart*. London: Thames & Hudson, 1961.
16 Solzhenitsyn (Alexander) *One Day in the Life of Ivan Denisovich*. London: Gollancz, 1962.
17 Quaker Women's Group, *Bringing the Invisible into the Light: Some Quaker Feminists speak of their experience* (Swarthmore Lecture 1986) London: QHS, 1986.
18 Gorman, op. cit.

CHAPTER 4
1 Jung (C. G.) *Psychology and Religion* (Collected Works Vol. 11) p. 264.
2 Ibid.
3 *Psychological Reflections*, op. cit., p. 240 or Ark edn., p. 271.

[4] *CFP*, op. cit., §120. Drafted by the 1925 Revision Committee.
[5] *Psychological Reflections*, op. cit., p. 317 or Ark edn., p. 353.
[6] Eddington (Arthur S.) *Science and the Unseen World* (Swarthmore Lecture 1929). London: Allen & Unwin, 1929, pp. 53–6. Quoted in *CFP*, op. cit., §124.
[7] Ibid.
[8] James, op. cit., p. 476.
[9] Gorman, op. cit., p. 31.
[10] Eddington, op. cit., p. 50. Quoted in *CFP* §140.
[11] *Psychological Reflections*, op. cit., p. 308 or Ark edn. p. 346.
[12] *Jung: Selected Writings*, op. cit., p. 391.
[13] Gorman, op. cit., p. 58.
[14] Ibid.
[15] Ibid.
[16] Ibid.
[17] Knight (Francis H.). 'The Faith of a Sceptic' in *Wayfarer* vol. 24 (1945) pp. 110–11. Quoted in *CFP* §107.
[18] Matthews (John) *The Grail: Quest for the Eternal*. London: Thames & Hudson, 1981, p. 5.
[19] Wilkins (Eithne) *The Rose Garden Game*. London: Gollancz, 1969.
[20] Gorman, op. cit., p. 58.
[21] Matthews, op. cit., p. 5.
[22] Olden (Ole) letter in *The Friend*, vol. 113, 1955, p. 1026. Quoted in *CFP* §125.
[23] Eddington, op. cit., pp. 53–56. Quoted in *CFP*, §124.
[24] Ibid.
[25] Wood (Herbert G.) article in *Birmingham Post* 26 November 1955. Quoted *CFP*, §126.
[26] Jones (Rufus M.) 'The Spiritual Message of the Religious Society of Friends' in *Report of the Commission I* of the World Conference of Friends, 1937. Quoted *CFP* §244.
[27] Hetherington (Ralph) *The Sense of Glory* (Swarthmore Lecture 1975) London: Quaker Home Service, 1975. p. 26.
[28] Macmurray (John) 'What is Religion?' in *The Listener*, 13 December 1956.
[29] Gorman, op. cit., p. 38.
[30] Kee (Alastair) *The Way of Transcendence*. Harmondsworth, Middx: Penguin, 1971, p. 18. Quoted by George Gorman, op. cit., p. 60.
[31] Gorman, op. cit., p. 60.
[32] *Jung: Selected Writings*, op. cit., p. 329.
[33] Ibid.
[34] Ibid., p. 240.
[35] *Memories, Dreams, Reflections*, op. cit., p. 415.
[36] Koestler (Arthur) *The Act of Creation*. London: Hutchinson, 1964.
[37] *Psychological Reflections*, op. cit., p. 179 or Ark edn., p. 199.
[38] Clark (Kenneth) *Civilisation*. London: BBC and John Murray, 1969, pp. 1, 3, 14, 17, 201, 251, 346.
[39] *Memories, Dreams, Reflections*, op. cit., p. 415.
[40] Williams (H.A.) *The True Resurrection*. London: Constable, 1965, pp.92 and 173.
[41] Ibid., p. 174.
[42] Hetherington, op. cit., p. 65.
[43] Gorman, op. cit., p. 71.

[44] *Psychological Reflections* op. cit., p. 203.
[45] Ibid., p. 208.
[46] Ibid., p. 209.
[47] Ibid., p. 199.
[48] 'Epistle of London Yearly Meeting 1879' in *Yearly Meeting Proceedings,* 1879, pp. 38–9. Quoted in *CFP* §170.
[49] Bosanquet (Ellen S.) *The Inward Light,* 1927, p. 6. Quoted in *CFP* §182.
[50] Greenwood (John Ormerod) *Signs of Life* (Swarthmore Lecture 1978) London: Quaker Home Service, 1978.
[51] Parker-Rhodes (Damaris) *Truth: A Path and Not a Possession* (Swarthmore Lecture 1977) London: Quaker Home Service, 1977.
[52] Ibid. Quoted by Greenwood op. cit., p. 62.
[53] Fox. *Journal* op. cit., p. 263. Quoted in *CFP* §376.
[54] *Church Government* op. cit., §702 III.

CHAPTER 5
[1] Cuppitt (Don) *The Sea of Faith.* London: BBC, 1984, p. 176.
[2] *Church Government* op. cit., §702 III.
[3] Ibid.
[4] *Jung: Selected Writings* op. cit., p. 380.
[5] Ibid., p. 397.
[6] Ibid., p. 322.
[7] Ibid., p. 299.
[8] Ibid.
[9] Ibid., p. 258.
[10] *Psychological Reflections* op. cit., p. 318.
[11] Browning (Robert) 'Bishop Blougram's Apology' line 666 in *Poetical Works of Robert Browning 1833–1864.* London: Oxford University Press, 1970, p. 663.
[12] *Psychological Reflections* op. cit., p. 318 or Ark edn., p. 354.
[13] In conversation.
[14] *Psychological Reflections* op. cit., p. 317 or Ark edn. p. 352.
[15] Ibid., p. 194 or Ark edn. p. 216.
[16] *Jung: Selected Writings* op. cit., p. 366.
[17] Küng (Hans) *On being a Christian,* London: Collins (Fount Paperbacks) 1978, p. 380.
[18] Ibid.
[19] *Jung: Selected Writings* op. cit., p. 366.
[20] Gorman, op. cit., pp. 99–122.
[21] Tolstoy (Leo) *Resurrection* trns. Rosemary Edmonds. Harmondsworth, Middx: Penguin, 1966, p. 185.
[22] Küng, op. cit., p. 380.
[23] Wittgenstein (Ludwig) *Culture and Value,* 1980. Quoted by Don Cuppitt, op. cit., p. 223.
[24] Küng, op. cit., p. 380.
[25] Cuppitt, op. cit., p. 258.
[26] Harvey (John W.) *The Salt and the Leaven* (Swarthmore Lecture 1947. London: Allen & Unwin, 1947, p. 37–8. Quoted in *CFP* §665.
[27] 'Friends and the Ecumenical movement' in *Friends face the fourth century.* Official Report of the World Conference of Friends, p. 54.
[28] Ibid.
[29] Cuppitt op. cit., p. 117.
[30] *Psychological Reflections* op. cit., p. 180 or Ark edn., p. 199.

[31] Shaw (George Bernard) *Saint Joan*. London: Constable, 1924, Scene 1.

CHAPTER 6
[1] Gorman op. cit., p. 58.
[2] *Matthew* 19:21 (AV).
[3] *Matthew* 19:21 (NEB).
[4] *Matthew* 5:48 (AV).
[5] *Matthew* 5:48 (NEB).
[6] *Luke* 6:36 (AV).
[7] Luke 6:36 (NEB).
[8] Peters (Richard) *Reason, Morality and Religion* (Swarthmore Lecture 1972) London: Quaker Home Service, 1972, p. 97.
[9] Ibid., p. 95.
[10] Ibid.
[11] Shakespeare (William) 'Twelfth Night' in *Complete Works* ed. by W. J. Craig, London: Oxford Univ. Press, 1928, Act II, iii: 124, p. 351.
[12] Peters op. cit., p. 97.
[13] Ibid., p. 87.
[14] Source untraced.
[15] Ibid.
[16] *Psychological Reflections* op. cit., p. 212. Cf. Ark edn., pp. 236–9.
[17] Ibid.
[18] *Jung: Selected Writings* op. cit., p. 269.

CHAPTER 7
[1] *Genesis* 2:9 (AV).
[2] *Jung: Selected Writings* op. cit., p. 25.
[3] Ibid., p. 141.
[4] Ibid., p. 142.
[5] Huxley (Aldous) *The Perennial Philosophy* London: Chatto & Windus, 1946 or Collins (Fontana), 1963, pp. 158–161.
[6] Sterne (Laurence) *Tristram Shandy*, Book 4, chapter 31. London: Oxford Univ. Press (Worlds Classics, rpt. 1961, p. 305).
[7] *Jung: Selected Writings* op. cit., p. 159.
[8] Ibid.
[9] Ibid., p. 167.
[10] Ibid.
[11] Ibid., p. 181.
[12] Ibid., p. 19.
[13] Ibid., p. 59.
[14] Bridges (Robert) *Testament of Beauty*. Oxford: Clarendon Press, 2nd edn., 1930, book 1, line 6.
[15] Rowntree (John Wilhelm) *Palestine notes and other papers*, 1906, p. 110. Quoted in *Church Government*, §852.
[16] Ibid.
[17] *Church Government* op. cit., §853.

CHAPTER 8
[1] *John* 1:1 (AV).
[2] Ibid., 1:14 (AV).
[3] I Peter 2:2 (AV).
[4] I John 1:1 (AV).
[5] Scott (Janet) *What Canst Thou Say?* (Swarthmore Lecture 1980) London: Quaker Home Service, 1980.

[6] Küng op. cit., p. 133.
[7] Jung (C. G.) *Jung Speaking* ed. by William McGuire and R. F. C. Hull. London: Thames & Hudson, 1978 or Pan Books (Picador) pp. 380–93. Interview on BBC 'Face to Face' by John Freeman.
[8] Ibid., p. 242. Interview with Frederick Sonds.
[9] *Jung: Selected Writings* op. cit., p. 324.
[10] Ibid.
[11] Ibid.
[12] Ibid., p. 329.
[13] Ibid., p. 392.
[14] Ibid.
[15] *Psychological Reflections* op. cit., p. 299 or Ark edn., p. 337.
[16] *Jung: Selected Writings* op. cit., p. 246.
[17] Ibid., p. 391.
[18] Peters op. cit. p. 85.
[19] *Psychological Reflections* op. cit., p. 271.
[20] Eddington op. cit., p. 50. Quoted in *CFP* §140.
[21] Ibid. Quoted in *CFP* §140.
[22] Scott op. cit., p. 76.
[23] Ibid.
[24] Ibid., p. 78.
[25] Ibid., p. 79.
[26] Ibid.
[27] Ibid.
[28] Ibid., p. 80.
[29] Ibid.
[30] Penington (Isaac) in *Early Quaker Writings 1650–1700* ed. by Hugh Barbour & Arthur Roberts. Grand Rapids, Mich., USA: Eerdman, 1973, p. 382. Quoted by Janet Scott, op. cit., p. 80.
[31] Scott, op. cit., p. 81.
[32] Ibid., p. 82.
[33] Ibid.
[34] Ibid.
[35] Ibid., p. 57.
[36] Ibid.
[37] Ibid., p. 77.
[38] Ibid., p. 53.
[39] Browning (Robert) 'Pippa Passes' in *Poetical Works of Robert Browning 1833–1864*. London: Oxford Univ. Press, 1970, lines 228–9, p. 327 (NB. Not to be taken as Browning's own view. See *The Oxford Companion to English Literature* ed. by Margaret Drabble, 5th edn., 1987, p. 767).
[40] Julian of Norwich, from the plaque in the Julian Cell, Norwich.
[41] *Psychological Reflections* op. cit., p. 313 or Ark edn., p. 346.
[42] *Jung: Selected Writings* op. cit., p. 23.
[43] *Matthew* 10:30 (NEB).
[44] *Jung: Selected Writings* op. cit., p. 301.
[45] Ibid.
[46] Ibid., p. 319.
[47] Ibid.
[48] *Genesis* 2:9 (AV).
[49] *Jung: Selected Writings* op. cit., p. 308.
[50] Ibid., p. 280.

[51] Ibid., p. 257.
[52] Ibid.
[53] Ibid., p. 204.
[54] Ibid.
[55] Ibid., p. 205.
[56] Ibid.

CHAPTER 9
[1] Milton (John) 'When I consider how my light is spent' (Sonnet XIX) in *Poetical Works* ed. by Helen Darbishire. London: Oxford Univ. Press, 1958, rptd. 1963, p. 437.
[2] Penn (William) *A Collection of the Works* (1682). Quoted in *CFP* §395.
[3] 'Individual Responsibility in a changing society' in *Preparatory document 7* for Industry and the Social Order Conference, 1958. Quoted in *CFP* §599.
[4] *CFP* op. cit.
[5] *Luke* 10:31, 2 (AV).
[6] 'Individual Responsibility in a changing society' op. cit., Quoted in *CFP* §599.
[7] Brain (W. Russell) *Man, Society and Religion* (Swarthmore Lecture 1944) London: Allen & Unwin, 1944. Quoted in *CFP* §141.
[8] *Psychological Reflections* op. cit., p. 220 or Ark edn., p. 249.
[9] *Jung: Selected Writings* op. cit., p. 253.
[10] Ibid., p. 203.
[11] Ibid., p. 199.
[12] Ibid.
[13] *Psychological Reflections* op. cit., p. 214 or Ark edn., p. 239.
[14] Ibid.
[15] *Jung: Selected Writings* op. cit., p. 197.
[16] Ibid.
[17] Ibid.
[18] *Psychological Reflections* op. cit., p. 215 or Ark edn., p. 240.
[19] *Jung: Selected Writings* op. cit., p. 198.
[20] Ibid.
[21] *Psychological Reflections* op. cit., p. 211 or Ark edn., p. 237.
[22] Ibid., p. 212.
[23] *Jung: Selected Writings* op. cit., p. 100.
[24] Ibid., p. 198.

CHAPTER 10
[1] *Jung: Selected Writings* op. cit., p. 221.
[2] Ibid., p. 101.
[3] *Psychological Reflections* op. cit., p. 100 or Ark edn., p. 113.
[4] Ibid., p. 94 or Ark edn., p. 105.
[5] The form of Soleminization of Matrimony in *Book of Common Prayer.* Cambridge Univ. Press.
[6] Shakespeare op. cit., Sonnet 116, p. 1299.
[7] *Psychological Reflections* op. cit., p. 100, or Ark edn., p. 113.
[8] *Jung: Selected Writings* op. cit., p. 415.
[9] *Letters of P. B. Shelley* ed. by F. L. Jones. London: Oxford Univ. Press, 1964, vol. 2, p. 434.
[10] *Psychological Reflections* op. cit., p. 100, or Ark edn., p. 115.
[11] Ibid., p. 97 or Ark edn., p. 110.

[12] *Jung: Selected Writings* op. cit., p. 414.
[13] *Psychological Reflections* op. cit., p. 99, or Ark edn., p. 112.
[14] *John* 1:14 (AV).
[15] *Psychological Reflections* op. cit., p. 106, or Ark edn., p. 122.
[16] Ibid., or Ark edn., p. 121.
[17] Ibid., p. 105 or Ark edn., p. 121.

CHAPTER 11
[1] Fox, *Journal*, op. cit. Quoted in *CFP* §5.
[2] Ibid. Quoted in *CFP* §20.
[3] *Church Government* §702 III.
[4] Ibid., Postcript 1656.
[5] Conrad (Joseph) *Lord Jim*. 1900. Harmondsworth, Middx: Penguin, 1987.
[6] Shakespeare (William) *Hamlet* ed. by Edward Dowden. London: Oxford Univ. Press (World's Classics), Act I, scene 5.
[7] *Matthew* 4:10 (AV) [NEB: 'Begone Satan'].
[8] *Oxford Companion to English Literature* op. cit., p. 787.

CHAPTER 12
[1] *I Corinthians* 13:11 (AV).
[2] *CFP* op. cit., §702 IV.
[3] *Jung: Selected Writings* op. cit., p. 203.
[4] Ibid., p. 198.
[5] Ibid.
[6] *Psychological Reflections* op. cit., p. 143.
[7] Ibid., p. 149 or Ark edn., p. 166.
[8] *Jung: Selected Writings* op. cit., p. 375.
[9] *Psychological Reflections* op.cit., p. 137 Ark edn., p. 155.
[10] Ibid., p. 149 or Ark edn. p. 166.
[11] *Jung: Selected Writings* op. cit., p. 202.
[12] Ibid, p. 354.
[13] Ibid., p. 403.
[14] Ibid., p. 201.
[15] *Psychological Reflections* op. cit., p. 149.
[16] *Jung: Selected Writings* op. cit., p. 375.
[17] Ibid., op. cit., p. 376.
[18] Shelley (P. B.) 'Lines Written among the Euganean Hills' in *Complete Poetical Works* ed. by Thomas Hutchinson. London: Oxford Univ. Press, 1905, rptd. 1948, Lines 231–235, p. 556.

CHAPTER 13
[1] *Church Government* op. cit., §702 I.
[2] Ibid., §702 II
[3] *Psychological Reflections* op. cit., p. 150 or Ark edn., p. 169.
[4] Ibid.
[5] *Jung: Selected Writings* op. cit., p. 277.
[6] Ibid.
[7] Ibid., p. 204.
[8] Ibid., p. 90.
[9] Ibid., p. 226.
[10] *Memories, Dreams, Reflections* op. cit., p. 370.
[11] Ibid.

[12] Ibid.
[13] *Genesis* 1:3 (AV).
[14] Shakespeare (William) 'Hamlet' in *Complete Works* ed. by W. J. Craig op. cit., III: 2:272, 3.
[15] *Genesis* 1:3 (AV).
[16] *John* 12:46 (AV).
[17] Fox, *Journal*, op. cit., p. 263. Quoted in *CFP* §376.
[18] *Jung: Selected Writings* op. cit., p. 116.
[19] Ibid., p. 25.
[20] Shelley (P. B.) 'Prometheus Unbound' in *Complete Poetical Works* ed. by Thomas Hutchinson. London: Oxford Univ. Press, 1905, rptd. 1948, Act 1, lines 190–202.
[21] de la Mare (Walter) 'Self to Self' in *Collected Works*. London: Faber, 1979, p. 186.
[22] *Jung: Selected Writings* op. cit., p. 403.

CHAPTER 14
[1] Underhill (Evelyn) *Mysticism*. London: Metheun, 1960, p. 222.
[2] *Psychological Reflections*, op. cit., p. 108 or Ark edn., p. 124.
[3] Plato. *The Republic*, Book VII. (various editions).
[4] Zola (Emile) *The Earth* trns. Douglas Parmee. Harmondsworth, Middx: Penguin Classics, 1980, p. 123.
[5] From the title of the 1986 Swarthmore Lecture, *Bringing the Invisible into the Light* op. cit.
[6] *Church Government* op. cit., §702 I.
[7] *Psychological Reflections* op. cit., p. 240 or Ark edn. p. 271.
[8] Shelley (P. B.) 'Adonais' in *Complete Poetical Works* ed. by Thomas Hutchinson. London: Oxford Univ. Press, 1905, rptd. 1948, Stanza LII, p. 443.
[9] *Church Government* op. cit., §702 II.
[10] Hunter (Elizabeth) quoted in *The Choice is Always Ours* ed. by Dorothy Berkley Phillips. Wheaton, Ill. USA: Theosophical Pub. House (Re-Quest Books) 1948, rev. rpt. 1975 now published by Harper Collins.
[11] Wordsworth (William) 'The Prelude' (1850) in *Poetical Works* ed. by Thomas Hutchinson. London: Oxford Univ. Press, 1904, new edn. 1967, p. 499, Book 1, lines 341–344.
[12] de la Mare (Walter) 'I Sit Alone' in *Collected Poems* op. cit., p. 175.

Bibliography

1 Alain-Fournier: *The Lost Domain (Le Grand Meaulnes)* tr Frank Davison. Oxford University Press (World's Classics), 1959 (f.p. 1913).
2 Barnes (Kenneth C.): *The Creative Imagination*. FHSC, 1967.
3 Bettelheim (Bruno): *The Informed Heart*. Thames & Hudson, 1961.
4 Bettelheim (Bruno): *The Uses of Enchantment*. Penguin (Peregrine Books), 1978.
5 *Bhagavad-Gita*, tr Swami Prabhavananda & Christopher Isherwood. Phoenix House, 1967 (f.p. 1947).
6 Bodkin (Maud): *Archetypal Patterns in Poetry*. Oxford University Press (Oxford Paperbacks), 1963.
7 Bridges (Robert) ed.: *The Spirit of Man* (anthology). Longmans Green & Co, 1915.
8 Brown (J. A. C.): *Freud and the Post-Freudians*. Penguin, 1961.
9 Bryant (Christopher): *The River Within*. Darton Longman & Todd, 1978.
10 Burnett (Frances Hodgson): *The Secret Garden*. Penguin (Puffin Classics), 1951 (f.p. 1911).
11 Castle (E.B.): *Approach to Quakerism*. Quaker Home Service, 1973, (f.p. 1961).
12 *Church Government*. London Yearly Meeting of the Religious Society of Friends, 1968.
13 *Christian Faith and Practice in the Experience of the Society of Friends*. London Yearly Meeting of the Religious Society of Friends, 1960.
14 *Cloud of Unknowing, The:* trans. Clifton Wolters. Penguin Classics, 1961. (A paraphrase of this book by Robert Backhouse was published by Hodder & Stoughton in 1958).
15 Cowen (Painton): *Rose Windows*. Thames & Hudson, 1979.
16 Cupitt (Don): *The Sea of Faith*. BBC, 1984.
17 *Dhammapada, The:* tr Juan Mascaro. Penguin, 1973.
18 Eddington (Arthur S.): *Science and the Unseen World*. Allen & Unwin, 1929.
19 Eliot, (T. S.): *The Cocktail Party*. Faber & Faber, 1950. (First public performance 1949).
20 Field (Joanna) [Marion Milner]: *A Life of One's Own*. Pelican, 1952.
21 *Folklore, Myths and Legends of Britain*. Reader's Digest Association, 1977.
22 Fordham (Frieda): *An Introduction to Jung's Psychology*. Penguin, 1959.
23 Freud (Sigmund); *Two Short Accounts of Psychoanalysis*. Pelican, 1962.
24 Freud (Sigmund): *An Outline of Psychoanalysis*. Hogarth Pess, 1949.
25 Gorman (George): *The Amazing Fact of Quaker Worship*. FHSC, 1973.
26 Greenwood (J. Ormerod): *Signs of Life*. FHSC, 1978.
27 Halmos (Paul): *The Faith of the Counsellors*. Constable, 1965.
28 Happold (F. C.): *Mysticism*. Pelican, 1963.
29 Hardy (Jean): *A Psychology with a Soul*. Routledge & Kegan Paul, 1987.

30 Hesse (Hermann): *The Glass Bead Game*. Penguin, 1972. (f.p. 1943).
31 Hesse (Hermann): *My Belief*. Triad Panther, 1979.
32 Hesse (Hermann): *Siddhartha*. Pan Books (Picador), 1973.
33 Hetherington (Ralph): *The Sense of Glory*. FHSC, 1975.
34 Hewitt (James): *Meditation*. Hodder & Stoughton (Teach Yourself Books), 1978.
35 Hick (John): *The Second Christianity*. SCM Press, 1968.
36 Hollitscher (Walter): *Sigmund Freud, an Introduction*. Kegan Paul, 1947.
37 Howes (Elizabeth B.) & Moon (Sheila): *The Choicemaker*. Theosophical Publishing House, Wheaton, Illinois, 1977.
38 Humphreys (Christmas): *Studies in the Middle Way*. Allen & Unwin, 1959.
39 Huxley (Aldous): *The Perennial Philosophy*. Collins (Fontana Books), 1958). (f.p. 1946).
40 Jacobi (Jolande) ed: *Psychological Reflections*. Pantheon Books, USA & Routledge & Kegan Paul , 1954. (Revised edition, Art Paperbacks, Routledge & Kegan Paul, 1986).
41 *The Way of Individuation*. Meridian Books, New American Library, New York, 1965.
42 James (William): *The Varieties of Religious Experience*. Collins (Fount Paperbacks) 1977. (Gifford Lectures 1901–2).
43 Jeffreys (M. V. C.): *Personal Values in the Modern World*. Pelican, 1962.
44 Johnson (Raynor C.): *A Religious Outlook for Modern Man*. Hodder & Stoughton, 1963.
45 Johnston (William): *The Inner Eye of Love*. Collins, Fount Paperbacks, 1978.
46 Johnston (William): *Silent Music*. Collins, (Fontana Books), 1974.
47 Jones (Rufus M.): *The Faith and Practice of the Quakers*. Methuen 1949. (f.p. 1927).
48 Jung (C.G.): *Analytical Psychology: Its Theory & Practice*. Routledge Paperbacks, 1968. (Tavistock Lecture 1935).
49 Jung (C. G.): *Answer to Job*. Hodder & Stoughton, 1965, Routledge & Kegan Paul, 1954.
50 Jung (C. G.): *The Development of Personality*. Pantheon Books (USA) and Routledge & Kegan Paul (UK) 1954. (Complete Works vol. 17).
51 Jung (C. G.): *Memories, Dreams, Reflections*. Fontana Paperbacks (Flamingo), 1983.
52 Jung (C. G.): *Modern Man in Search of a Soul*. Routledge & Kegan Paul, 1961. (f.p. 1933).
53 Jung (C. G.): *Psychology and Alchemy*. Pantheon Books (USA) and Routledge & Kegan Paul, 1968. (Completed Works vol. 12).
54 Jung (C. G.): *The Undiscovered Self*. Routledge & Kegan Paul, 1958.
55 *Jung Speaking*, edited William McGuire and R. F. C. Hull: Pan Books, (Picador) 1980.
56 Khan (J. H.): *Job's Illness*. Pergamon Press, 1975.
57 Kermode (Frank): *The Romantic Image*. Routledge & Kegan Paul, 1957.
58 Kirk (G.S.): *Greek Myths*. Pelican. 1974.
59 Klein (Melanie) and Riviere (Joan): *Love, Hate and Reparation*. Hogarth Press, 1953.
60 Koestler (Arthur): *The Act of Creation*. Hutchinson, 1964.

61 Kraemer (Hendrick): *World Cultures and World Religions*. Lutterworth Press, 1960.
62 Küng (Hans): *Does God Exist?* Collins (Fount Paperback) 1978.
63 Küng (Hans): *On Being a Christian*. Collins (Fount Paperback) 1978.
64 Lao Tzu: *Tao Te Ching*, trans D. C. Lan. Penguin Classics, 1984.
65 Leon (Philip): *Beyond Belief and Unbelief*. Gollancz, 1965.
66 Lewis (C. S.): *Christian Reflections*. Collins (Fount Paperbacks) 1981. (f.p. 1967).
67 Lewis (C. S.): *The Four Loves*. Collins (Fount Paperbacks) 1977.
68 Lewis (C.S.): *Prayer: Letters to Malcolm*. Collins (Fontana Books) 1966.
69 Lewis (C. S.): *Surprised By Joy*. Collins (Fount Paperbacks) 1959.
70 Lomas (Peter): *True and False Experience*. Allen & Unwin, 1973.
71 Lucas (F. L.): *The Decline and Fall of the Romantic Ideal*. Cambridge University Press, 1963 (f.p. 1936).
72 Macmurray (John): *Persons in Relation*. Faber, 1961.
73 Marlow (A. N.): *Radhakrishnan* (an anthology). Allen & Unwin, 1953.
74 Matthew (John): *The Grail: Quest for the Eternal*. Thames & Hudson, 1981.
75 May (Rollo): *The Courage to Create*. William Collins & Sons, 1975.
76 Otto (Rudolf): *The Idea of the Holy*. Trans John W. Harvey. Pelican, 1959. (f.p. 1917).
77 Otto (Rudolf): *Mysticism, East and West*. Meridian Books, New York, 1957.
78 Peters (Richard S.): *Reason, Mortality and Religion*. FHSC, 1972.
79 Philips (Dorothy Berkley) *The Choice is Always Ours*, an anthology. Re-Quest Books, Theosophical Publishing House, Wheaton, USA (1948). Revised ed. 1977; now published by Harper Collins.
80 Priestland (Gerald): *Yours Faithfully*. Collins (Fount Paperbacks) 1979.
81 Punshon (John): *Encounter With Science*. Friends United Press, Richmond, Indiana, USA and QHS, London, 1987.
82 Purce (Jill): *The Mystic Spiral*. Thames & Hudson, 1974.
83 Rogers (Carl R.): *Client-Centred Therapy*. London: Constable and USA: Houghton Mifflin Co. 1951.
84 Rudin (Josef): *Psychotherapy and Religion*. University of Notre Dame Press, Indiana, USA, 1968.
85 Russell (Peter): *Meditation*. BBC, 1978.
86 Rycroft (Charles) ed: *Psychoanalysis Observed*. (Various contributors). Constable, 1966.
87 Sanford (John A.): *Healing and Wholeness*, Paulist Press, New York, 1977.
88 Scott (Janet): *What Canst Thou Say?* QHS, 1980.
89 Spiegelberg (Frederic): *Living Religions of the World*. Thames & Hudson, 1957.
90 Stafford-Clark (D.): *What Freud Really Said*. Pelican, 1967.
91 Storr (Anthony) ed: *Jung—Selected Writings*. Fontana Paperbacks, 1983.
92 Storr (Anthony): *The Integrity of the Personality*. Penguin, 1960.
93 Teilhard de Chardin (Pierre): *The Future of Man*. Collins, (Fontana Books) 1969.
94 Teilhard de Chardin (Pierre): *The Phenomenon of Man*. Collins, 1959.

95 Thouless (Robert H.): *The Psychology of Religion.* Cambridge University Press, 1961 (f.p. 1923).
96 Tillich (Paul): *The Courage To Be.* Collins, 1962.
97 Tolstoy (Leo): *A Confession and What I Believe.* Oxford University Press, World's Classics, 1921 reprinted with *The Gospel in Brief* 1940 (f.p. 1882 and 1884).
98 Tolstoy (Leo): *The Kingdom of God & Peace Essays.* Oxford University Press, World's Classics, 1936 (f.p. 1893).
99 Tolstoy (Leo): *Resurrection.* trans. Rosemary Edwards. Penguin, 1966.
100 Underhill (Evelyn): *Mysticism.* University Paperbacks, Methuen, 1960 (f.p. 1930).
101 Underhill (Evelyn): *Worship.* Nisbet & Co, 1936.
102 Watts (Alan W.): *Myth and Ritual in Christianity.* Thames & Hudson, 1954.
103 Wiles (Maurice): *Faith and the Mystery of God.* SCM Press, 1982.
104 Wilkins (Eithne) *The Rose Garden Game.* Gollancz, 1969.
105 Williams (H. A.): *Theology and Self-Awareness.* (Essay in *Soundings,* ed. A. R. Vidler). Cambridge University Press, 1962.
106 Williams (H. A.): *True Resurrection.* Mitchell Beazley, 1972.
107 Williams (H. A.): *The True Wilderness.* Constable, 1965.
108 Wilson (John): *Religion.* Heinemann Educational Books, 1972.
109 Yungblutt (John R.): *Discovering God Within.* Westminster Press, Philadelphia, USA, 1979.

Editorial Revisions for the Second Edition

Page 8 end of 4th paragraph: a reference to Christian Faith and Practice: *Christian Faith and Practice* and *Church Government* have been subsumed into the new Quaker Book of Discipline: *Quaker faith and practice.* This has a chapter entitled 'General Counsel on Church Affairs'.

Page 27, line 1. We would now ask how does any parent cope with sick and distressed child . . .

Page 93: References to the Book of Discipline would now be Chapter 2 of *Quaker faith and practice.*

Page 111 and 112: References to personal relationship and to the unconscious are much stronger in *Quaker faith and practice*—see Chapters 21 and 22.

Amended References for the Second Edition

Page 191 Chapter 1, No. 20: In 1995, Britain Yearly Meeting issued its most recent Book of Discipline, now called *Quaker faith and practice: The book of Christian discipline of the Yearly Meeting of the Religious Society of Friends in Britain*. Britain Yearly Meeting, 1995. This is the principal contemporary Quaker book for British Friends. In the new book, there are no references to evil itself but the references to dark and darkness now outnumber those to light. in *Quaker faith and practice* there are 30 indexed references to dark and darkness and 15 to light.

Page 193 No. 22: The reference to Ole Olden is also found in *Quaker faith and practice* 26.17.

Page 194. No. 48: The reference from the Epistle of London Yearly Meeting 1879 is also found in *Quaker faith and practice* 26.63.

Page 194 No. 49: The reference from Ellen S Bosanquet is also found in *Quaker faith and practice* 26.68.

Page 194 No. 53: The reference from *The Journal* of George Fox is also found in *Quaker faith and practice* 19.32.

Page 194 No. 54: A similar sentiment, with slightly different wording, can be found in *Quaker faith and practice* 1.02.7.

Page 194 No. 2: See also *Quaker faith and practice* 1.02.2.

Page 195 No. 15: Again note that *Quaker faith and practice* now includes Church Government material.

Page 197 No. 2 Chapter 9, No. 2: The reference from William Penn is also found in *Quaker faith and practice* 21.17.

Page 198 Chapter 11 No. 1: This reference from *The Journal* of George Fox is also found in *Quaker faith and practice* 19.02.

Page 198 No. 2: This reference from *The Journal* of George Fox is also found in *Quaker faith and practice* 19.07.

Page 198 No. 3: See also *Quaker faith and practice* 1.02.7.

Page 198 No. 4: See also *Quaker faith and practice* 1.01.

Page 198: In the new Quaker Book of Discipline, Love, Kindness, Compassion and Sex are not mentioned. Sexuality has 20 indexed references and Sin, 13.

Page 198 Chapter 12 No. 2: See also *Quaker faith and practice* 1.02.27.

Page 198 Chapter 13 No. 1: See also *Quaker faith and practice* 1.02.3.

Page 198 No. 2: See also *Quaker faith and practice* 1.02.9.

Page 199 No. 17: This reference from *The Journal* of George Fox is also found in *Quaker faith and practice* 19.32.

Page 199 No. 6: See also *Quaker faith and practice* 1.02.18.

Page 199 No. 9: See also *Quaker faith and practice* 1.02.9.

Page 204: In 1999 we would consider *Quaker faith and practice: The book of Christian discipline of the Yearly Meeting of the Religious Society of Friends in Britain*, Britain Yearly Meeting, 1995 as the prime Quaker reference.

Suggested reading on Quaker topics

Quaker faith and practice: The book of Christian discipline of the Yearly Meeting of the Religious Society of Friends (Quakers) in Britain, Britain Yearly Meeting 1995 (83).

A Light that is Shining, Harvey Gillman, Quaker Home Service, 1997.

General Index

References are to pages

210

Shakespeare's sonnets 28
Shaw (G. B.) 68, 99
Sheldon (W. H.) 84, 85
Shelley (P. B.) 130, 160, 176, 187
Society of Friends 68, 96
Solzhenitsin (A.) 36
Stekel (W.) 83
Sterne (L.) 86
Storr (A.) 8, 10, 20, 60, 83, 104, 176
Summun bonum 106, 107

Tao 88
Taoists 39
Taoism 33
Tavistock Institute 16
therapist 22, 23, 90, 97, 149, 183
  (see also psychotherapist)
therapy 38, 87, 93, 189
  (see also psychotherapy)
thinking 131, 150, 164
Thompson (F.) 47
Tolstoy (L.) 65, 98
transcendence 45, 46, 53, 101, 156, 166, 176, 177, 187
transcendent function 170, 175

Trinity, the 10, 102
  doctrine of 103
True Resurrection 52, 64

Ulverston 137
Underhill (E.) 180
Undiscovered Self, The 104
United States 17
Universalists 187

vocation 53, 54, 66, 113, 114, 116, 143, 153, 156, 157, 161–165, 177, 181

Wetherhead (L.) 16
Williams (H. A.) 52, 53, 64
Wittgenstein (L.) 66
Wood (H. G.) 46
Wordsworth (W.) 189

Yahweh 106

Zen 54, 181, 188
Zola (E.) 181
Zoroaster 181

Jung Quotations

References are to page numbers